GETTING
THINGS
DONE

Also by Edwin C. Bliss

DOING IT NOW

GETTING THINGS DONE

The ABCs of Time Management

EDWIN C. BLISS

Futura

A Futura Book

Copyright © 1976 by Edwin C. Bliss

Illustrations by Malcolm Hancock

First published in Great Britain in 1985
by Futura Publications, a Division of
Macdonald & Co (Publishers) Ltd
London & Sydney
Reprinted 1986, 1987

ISBN 0 7088 2731 4

Printed and bound in Great Britain by
Collins, Glasgow

Futura Publications
A Division of
Macdonald & Co (Publishers) Ltd
Greater London House
Hampstead Road
London NW1 7QX

A BPCC plc Company

To Libby,
who practices what I preach

There is nothing which I wish more that you should know, and which fewer people do know, than the true use and value of time. It is in everybody's mouth, but in few people's practice. Every fool, who slatterns away his whole time in nothing, utters, however, some trite commonplace sentence, of which there are millions, to prove, at once, the value and the fleetness of time. The sun-dials all over Europe have some ingenious inscriptions to that effect; so that nobody squanders away their time without hearing and seeing daily how necessary it is to employ well, and how irrecoverable it is if lost.

Lord Chesterfield
Letters to His Son

CONTENTS

GETTING THINGS DONE

INTRODUCTION

I first became interested in patterns of time use many years ago, when, as an assistant to a United States senator, I was struck with similarities in the operating styles of the more successful members of Congress. Faced with urgent and conflicting demands on their time—for committee work, floor votes, roll calls, speeches, ceremonies, interviews, briefings, correspondence, investigations, constituents' problems, and above all, the need to be informed on a wide range of unrelated subjects—they develop techniques for getting maximum benefit from minimum investments of time. They learn to set priorities in relation to their own goals rather than someone else's; they learn to screen themselves from unwarranted interruptions; they learn to delegate, to plan, to concentrate on important things, and to disregard trivia. If they don't learn, they don't return.

More recently, as a lobbyist for industry, I have worked with top executives of hundreds of corporations. Again, I have been impressed by the way the more successful ones always seem to have ample time for important matters, such as planning, and manage to stave off intrusions and activities that are nonproductive or trivial. It is true that they have more opportunity than most people to delegate time-consuming tasks, but that is only part of the reason for their effectiveness. They think in terms of objectives rather than activities; they make most decisions quickly; they speak and write concisely; they avoid procrastination; they treat their time as the precious and limited resource that it is.

As I became more conscious of time use, I began to apply in my own life some of the techniques I had observed, realizing that I was not one of those favored few to whom effective time use came naturally; and when I found how much more I could accomplish, I decided to write this book. The subjects are listed alphabetically, but if you'd prefer to begin with an overview of what time management is all about I'd suggest that you start with "Categories of Time Use."

Incidentally, most of the examples used in this book relate to the office, but I hope you won't take that to mean that these concepts are useful only in business. The principles of time management are universal, and they apply in any setting. For example, the techniques that can make corporate board meetings more effective are the same techniques that will put life into the meetings of the social committee of a square-dance club.

Before you begin, think for a moment about time. Could you define it? Probably not. The best my American Heritage Dictionary could come up with is "a nonspatial continuum in which events occur in apparently irreversible succession," which I don't find very helpful. I much prefer Ben Franklin's well-known definition: "Time is the stuff of which life is made."

If you will begin thinking of it in those terms, you are already on your way toward some drastic changes in the way you live . . . from this moment on.

AFTER-ACTION REPORTS

When your annual meeting is over, before you pack up all the unused brochures and settle your account with the catering manager, sit down in a quiet corner and make two lists: (1) everything you did right, and (2) everything you did wrong. Then put it in the file for next year's convention.

The military calls this an after-action report, and it's one bit of military red tape that is worthwhile and should be adopted by any organization of any size. Such a report should be made on any significant activity that is going to recur in the future, whether it's a meeting, a corporate acquisition, or a backpack trip. Memory is treacherous, and a year from now you will have forgotten the valuable lessons you learned this time around.

Your brief written record of what happened and why, including recommendations for how to do it better and more quickly next time, can save a lot of time and energy.

ALCOHOL

Drinking before lunch is a good way to transform early-afternoon prime time into secondary time. Alcohol is a depressant, and if you use it in the middle of the work day, you are diminishing your effectiveness.

But it relaxes you, you say. True. But in midday this kind of relaxation is the last thing you need.

A secondary effect of a drink before lunch is that it sharpens the appetite, causing you to order a heavier lunch than you would otherwise—compounding the problem of afternoon lethargy.

The head of one advertising agency dealt with the problem by calling his staff together and saying, "It has come to my attention that quite a few of you make it a practice to have a three-martini lunch. I want you to know that I have no objection to this—what you do on your lunch hour is your own business—but I would appreciate it if you would have those martinis made with gin rather than vodka. I realize that vodka is a little more difficult to detect on the breath—but that's just the point. When you call on our clients in the afternoon, I'd much rather have them think you're drunk than stupid!"

The old navy custom of refraining from drinking until the sun is over the yardarm is still a sound policy.

BEHAVIOR MODIFICATION

Misuse of time seldom involves an isolated incident; it usually is part of a well-established pattern of behavior, and to change for the better we often must grapple with a habit that has been developed over a period of many years.

There are two ways to change behavior patterns. One (described in the section on procrastination) involves forcing yourself to practice the new behavior pattern until it becomes ingrained. The other involves gradually "shaping" behavior through a system of rewards, the behavior-modification technique generally associated with B. F. Skinner of Harvard.

If you were to go all the way with behavior mod, you would plot carefully, perhaps on a logarithmic graph, the specific habits you wanted to reinforce or extinguish so that you could accurately measure your progress. And you might want to try aversion techniques, which cause undesired acts to evoke unpleasant associations.

For most of us, though, the important thing to learn is that *any behavior that is followed by something pleasant tends to be reinforced and is more likely to happen again.* You can get this reinforcement from others, but you can also reinforce your own behavior by giving yourself some kind of token reward for accomplishing (or starting or sticking with) a difficult or tedious task; staying with a priority item instead of getting sidetracked on a secondary job; getting started on an unpleasant task; turning down an unimportant but time-consuming request. The reward can be something trivial, so long as it has pleasant connotations. It can be tangible—a stick of gum, a drink of water, a snack. It could be giving yourself permission to do something—taking a break, or leaving work a little early, or buying a pair of shoes. Or it can consist of nothing more than giving yourself a mental pat on the back every time you take a small step in the right direction.

Two points to keep in mind: (1) punishing yourself for goofing is not nearly as effective as rewarding yourself for success, because positive reinforcement is by far the most effective way of changing behavior; and (2) you must reward yourself for each *small* success, not just for major achievements. If you start working on your income tax but soon get tired and quit, don't punish yourself for your failure—instead, reward yourself for having started the task. Then contrive another token reward to give yourself when you get started again.

BOTTLENECKS

A bottleneck can occur in an organization of any size whenever a key person fails to take an essential action, whether because of indecision, laziness, mistaken priorities, stubbornness, or overwork. It is a time-management problem of the greatest magnitude, since it wastes the time of an entire group of people.

Typical bottlenecks are caused by the corporation executive who refuses to say yes or no to a new idea; the bureaucrat who demands unnecessary paper work before approving a project; the club social committee which can't decide the details of a dance far enough in advance to give the decoration committee time to do a good job; the boss who delights in finding trivial imperfections in typing and demands that letters be done over; the teacher who waits until the last possible day to assign term papers; the boss who insists on being consulted on every decision made by subordinates but frequently isn't available for such consultations. The list is interminable. Most people don't realize how much they thwart the efforts of subordinates and co-workers by failing to respect their time needs.

While a bottleneck can result from a person having too much to do, it can also result from not having enough to do. In that situation, many people hoard paper work, building up a backlog to convince others (and often themselves) that they are busy. Like a tightwad nursing a drink in a nightclub, they can nurse a project indefinitely, giving the impression that something is happening. In such a case the solution is to give them more to do, not less, and set deadlines. This often works amazingly well as a purgative for a clogged pipeline.

If you are a victim of perpetual time binds because of an inept boss or an immovable bureaucracy, there may be little you can do about it, but at least you can try. Squawk. Nag. Cajole. Remind. Phone. Write memos. Keep in mind that to get anything done in this world, you often must be willing to be a bit obnoxious.

If you are an executive or a supervisor, the first place to look for bottlenecks is on your own desk, in your own "Pending" file, on your own "To Do" list, keeping in mind that, as someone has observed, bottlenecks are usually found at the tops of bottles. Get that paper work off your desk and on someone else's.

BREAKS

To work for long periods without taking a break is not an effective use of time. Energy decreases, boredom sets in, and physical stress and tension accumulate when a person stays with one thing too long. Irritability, chronic fatigue, headache, anxiety, and apathy all can be caused by failure to provide a change of pace during the working day.

A break need not be a "rest" break—indeed, switching to a different kind of work often can provide as much relief from tension as simply relaxing. Switching for a few minutes from a mental task to something physical can provide such a break. Walking around the office or around the block can serve as a quick restorative break. Changing from a sitting position to a standing position for a while can break up the monotony and provide some physical stimulus. Isometric exercises —tensing various muscles and working them against each other—can be done at your desk and are a good way to get a break from work.

Merely resting, however, is often the best course, and you should not think of a restorative break as poor use of time. Not only will being refreshed increase your efficiency, but relieving tension will benefit your health. Anything that contributes to health is good time management.

BRIEFCASE

The first-grader asked his mother why Daddy brought home a briefcase full of papers every evening. She explained, "It's because Daddy has so much to do he can't finish at the office and has to work nights." "Well, then," said the child, "why don't they just put him in a slower group?"

If you are an executive, you occasionally will have to take work home with you. That's the price you pay for the perquisites of office. However, if you find yourself doing it on a regular basis, it's a sign that something is wrong; either you are trying to do too many things yourself (see "Delegation"), or you have failed to organize your time at work effectively. A third possibility is that you may be suffering from a martyr complex and are trying to impress your associates or your family with how overworked you are (see "Workaholic").

You need to get away from work at the end of the day, both mentally and physically. Except in emergencies, time spent at home doing office work tends to be counterproductive, draining your energies and alienating your family. The homework habit also can dampen your drive to get things done at the office, because you tell yourself, "If I don't get this finished today, there's always tonight."

It isn't worth it. The only justification for taking

your briefcase home every evening is that you intend to use it the following morning for transporting your lunch.

CATEGORIES OF TIME USE

Action can be broken down into five categories: Important and Urgent, Important but not Urgent, Urgent but not Important, Busy Work, and Wasted Time.

1. *Important and Urgent*

These are the tasks that *must* be done, immediately or in the near future. Examples: Your boss demands a certain report by 10 A.M. tomorrow. Or your engine blows a gasket. Or the labor pains are three minutes apart. Or it's April 15 and you haven't finished your income tax form.*

Now, unless these situations all develop simultaneously (God forbid!) you can cope with them. Because of their urgency and their importance, they take precedence over everything else, and procrastination, if

---

* This is an example of a task that began in Category 2 and escalated to Category 1 now that you have reached the deadline.

a factor, is no longer possible. It is not here that we find our time management problems.

2. *Important but not Urgent*

Attention to this category is what divides effective individuals from ineffective ones.

Most of the really important things in our lives are not urgent. They can be done now or later. In many cases they can be postponed forever, and in too many cases they are. These are the things we "never get around to."

Examples: that special course you want to take to upgrade your professional skills; that new project you would like to suggest to your boss after you find time to do the preliminary fact-finding; that article you've been meaning to write; that diet you've intended to begin; that annual medical checkup you've planned to get for the past three years; that visit to a lawyer to have your will drawn; that retirement program you've been planning to establish.

All of these tasks have one thing in common: despite their importance, affecting as they do your health, your wealth, and your family's welfare, they will be postponed indefinitely unless you yourself initiate action. If your activities are keyed to other people's priorities, or to system-imposed deadlines that make things "urgent," you will never get around to your own priorities.

3. *Urgent but not Important*

In this category are those things that clamor for immediate action, but that we would assign a low priority if we examined them objectively.

For example, someone asks you to chair a fund drive or to give a speech or to attend a meeting. You might consider each of these low priority, but someone is standing in front of you waiting for an answer and you accept because you cannot think of a graceful way to decline. Then, because these tasks have built-in time limits, they get done, while Category 2 items get moved to the back burner.

4. *Busy Work*

There are many tasks that are marginally worth doing but are neither urgent nor important. We often do them ahead of more important things because they are *diversionary*—they provide a feeling of activity and accomplishment while giving us an excuse to put off tackling those Category 2 tasks which have far greater benefit.

One aerospace executive, for example, told me of coming to his office the previous Saturday morning to do some work he had been postponing. He decided to organize the materials on his desk. Having done so, he decided that while he was at it he might as well straighten up the desk drawers. He spent the rest of the morning reorganizing drawers and files.

"I left the office feeling vaguely disappointed that I hadn't accomplished what I went in for," he said, "but I consoled myself with the thought that I had been very busy doing some worthwhile things. I was playing games with myself—working on low-priority tasks, to give myself an excuse for further delay on the far more essential task I originally had assigned myself."

If you find time constantly being diverted by minutiae, try following the advice in the section on procrastination.

5. *Wasted Time*

The definition of wasted time is subjective, of course.

Ernest Hemingway is quoted as having defined "immoral" as "anything you feel bad after." I don't know whether that definition will stand up to theological scrutiny, but I do think it can be applied to wasted time. Television viewing, for example, can be time well spent if we come away feeling that we have been enlightened or entertained. But if, afterward, we feel that the time would have been better spent mowing the lawn or playing tennis or reading a good book, then we can chalk up that time as wasted.*

People who scramble madly to get control of their time often look in vain for things in this category upon which to blame their inefficiency. I am convinced, however, that with most people this is not where the problem lies. It lies rather with allocating too much time to things in Categories 3 and 4 rather than to those in Category 2.

* By any sane person's standards, about 95 percent of all television viewing must be put in this category, which is something to think about next time you reach for that knob.

CLUTTER

Some people use clutter as a sorting device. They have a constant swirl of papers on their desks and operate on the assumption that somehow the most important

matters will float to the top. This seems to work fairly well for some, and if it works I'm not going to knock it. Such people can feel straitjacketed if required to keep a tidy desk.*

But in most cases, clutter works the opposite way. It hinders concentration on a single task, because your eye is constantly diverted by other things. Clutter can create tension and frustration, a feeling of being disorganized and "snowed under."

Whenever you find your desk becoming chaotic, take time out to reorganize. Make a single pile of all your papers, then go through them (making generous

---

* Usually, however, people who get things done despite a chaotic desk are able to do so only because they have a secretary or an assistant whose orderliness compensates for their own disorganization.

use of your wastebasket) and divide them into categories:

1. Immediate action
2. Low priority
3. Pending
4. Reading material

Put the highest-priority item from your first pile in the center of your desk, then put everything else out of sight, either on a side table or in your desk. The temptation is to leave other high-priority items on your desk so you won't overlook them. But remember, you can think of only one thing at a time, and you can work on only one task at a time, so select the most important one and focus all your attention on it.

Essential to any office is some method of bringing things up automatically on specific dates. A calendar pad is helpful, but probably the best method is use of an accordion file with a pocket for each day of the month, and pockets for subsequent months. Or file folders can be set up in this manner, and kept in the desk. For offices handling a large volume of paper work, of course, more elaborate systems must be set up.

Clearing the desk completely, or at least organizing it, before leaving the office each evening should be standard practice. It gets the next day off to a good start.

A word about knickknacks—family photos, souvenir paperweights, clocks, thermometers, and other trinkets. Why not put them on a shelf, or on a side table, instead of on your desk, where they won't take up valuable working space and create visual distraction?

COMMUNICATION

A frequent cause of time waste is a lack of clear, direct, germane communication between people.

When Voltaire said, "Words were given to man to enable him to conceal his true feelings," he was describing the world as it too often is rather than as it should be. Too often we communicate with our boss, our fellow workers, or our subordinates in terms of what we think we *should* say, or in terms of what we think the other person would like to hear, instead of expressing our real feelings. We pussyfoot and call it tact. We equivocate and call it human relations. We offer mild praise for an unsatisfactory job a subordinate hands us, resolving to put the finishing touches on ourselves, instead of explaining that we had expected something different.

A mollycoddling attitude toward subordinates or a pussyfooting demeanor with superiors wastes the time of everyone involved. Open, frank communication is better for everyone concerned, keeping the air clear, avoiding a lot of time-wasting wheel-spinning.

This is not to say that tact doesn't have its place. The basic rule to keep in mind when communicating dissatisfaction is to talk about the *thing* rather than the *person*. Telling an employee he or she is not doing well is far less helpful than analyzing specific shortcomings in the project turned in.

The important thing is to make sure that sloppy

work by a subordinate does not go unchallenged, because that will increase your own work load and add to your time-management problems.

A clear statement of what is expected can save a lot of time for everyone concerned. If a subordinate's actions are wasting your time, your best bet is to say so simply and directly. Make it clear to subordinates (and superiors) that you are serious about making the best possible use of your time and need their help.

COMMUTE TIME

In large metropolitan areas, it is quite common to spend an hour on the highway or the commuter train getting to work in the morning, and another hour getting home. The average commute time in the United States is 22 minutes each way, and in metropolitan areas of a million or more population, 32 percent of commuters live more than 35 minutes from work.*

Anything that takes that much time out of your

* Nationwide Personal Transportation Study, Report No. 3, *Home-to-Work Trips and Travel*, published by U.S. Department of Transportation/Federal Highway Administration, August 1973.

life deserves special attention. Obviously, there are two things to consider: (1) Can commute time be reduced? And (2) can commute time be used more effectively?

Mr. Jones drives 35 minutes to get to work. His friend, Mr. Brown, lives only 15 minutes from the office. Mr. Jones doesn't think of the difference as being very significant—"only a few more miles, and you get used to it." But do the arithmetic: that 20-minute difference means 40 minutes a day, or 3⅓ hours per week. Figuring a 40-hour work week, Mr. Jones spends *four weeks more than Mr. Brown every year* in actual driving time!

Commute time should not be the overriding consideration in selecting a home, of course, but it deserves far more consideration than the average family gives it. A difference of "only" five or ten minutes can be a big difference indeed when figured on a cumulative basis. And the energy shortage, of course, gives everyone an added incentive to take a long, hard look at commuting distances.

As for the second point, the most effective use of commute time varies with each person. Listening to whatever happens to be on the car radio is seldom the best way to spend this time. More productive use might include: getting your thoughts in order before a morning staff meeting; analyzing business or personal problems or opportunities; mentally planning your day; listening to cassette tapes designed to increase professional skills. But it may be that listening to radio news or relaxing to a music tape would be the best use of time at that moment.

The important thing is to avoid using commute

time in a way determined by inertia or by habit. Consciously decide how you would prefer to channel your attention during the trip. You'll be surprised at how much real value can be obtained from those otherwise wasted moments.

CONCENTRATION

Of all the principles of time management, none is more basic than concentration. In counseling people who are having serious time-management problems, I find invariably that they are trying to do too many things simultaneously. When I insist that they must take them up one at a time they say, "But they are *all* important." And sometimes they are. But they can't be done simultaneously (unless some of them can be delegated, which of course is always worth considering).

The amount of time spent on a project is not what counts: it's the amount of *uninterrupted* time. Few problems can resist an all-out attack; few can be solved piecemeal.

Successful authors learn the importance of concentration. One of the most prolific of modern novelists was the French detective story writer Georges Simenon. Simenon's method was to cut himself off completely from the outside world while working on a book: no phone calls, no visitors, no newspapers, no mail; living, as he said, "like a monk." After about eleven days of total immersion in his writing he would emerge with another best-selling novel.

Few of us would carry concentration to that extreme—but if we did, who knows what we might accomplish?

Of course, under some circumstances doing two things at once—"killing two birds with one stone"—makes sense. But some people carry this concept to an extreme in their frantic efforts to get maximum value out of every minute. For example, in one of his famous letters to his son, dated December 11, 1747, Lord Chesterfield said:

> I knew a gentleman who was so good a manager of his time that he would not even lose that small portion of it which the calls of nature obliged him to pass in the necessary house; but gradually went through all the Latin poets in those moments. He bought, for example, a common edition of Horace, of which he tore off gradually a couple of pages, read them first, then sent them down a sacrifice to Cloacina; this was so much time fairly gained.

Well, perhaps. Personally, I believe good time management requires concentrating on one thing at a time, whether in the necessary house or elsewhere.

CONFERENCE CALLS

The most underused time-saving device, I am convinced, is the conference call.

In case you don't know (and it's surprising how many people don't), the conference call is simply a way of holding a meeting with any number of people, in almost any number of places, via telephone. You set it up simply by dialing o and giving the conference operator the names and phone numbers. Of course, it helps if you previously have alerted the people you intend to include, so they will be available and will have an idea of what is going to be discussed.

Many who use the conference call to bring together people in several different cities forget that it is equally valuable on a local basis. If you are a PTA president, for example, and have several items you must discuss briefly with your executive committee, you can either call a meeting, which kills the evening for everyone involved, or get everyone together on a conference call and conclude your business within a few minutes at a negligible cost.*

An incidental benefit of conference calls: when people know they are going to be charged by the minute, they tend to do their homework ahead of time and are much more concise in their discussion.

* At this writing, the cost of a four-party conference call in a typical American city is $1.80 for the first three minutes and 35¢ for each additional minute. A three-minute call linking New York, San Francisco, Chicago, and Atlanta is $8.50.

COPIES

Excessive record-keeping is a symptom of insecurity.

Figure out how often you use the various kinds of material you file. Take each category, and ask yourself, "What is the worst thing that could happen if this file didn't exist?" You'll find that most of the time the answer is "Nothing." If you really needed the information, it probably could be located elsewhere in the company in someone else's file. Or a phone call would do the trick, or you would get along fine without it.

This is not to say that comprehensive files aren't useful, but the question is whether they are useful *enough* to justify the amount of time and effort that goes into keeping them current. Estimate the amount of time spent filing such things as old company house organs, routine memoranda, information copies of other people's memos, and so on, and ask yourself if the company wouldn't be ahead if the same number of hours were put into something directed toward achieving your primary goal.

CORRESPONDENCE

How to handle correspondence quickly and efficiently:

1. Have incoming mail screened and sorted, if possible. If you open your own mail, sort as you open (with wastebasket close at hand).

2. Handle each letter only once. Avoid paper-shuffling. Do whatever has to be done (checking, forwarding, phoning, replying) immediately, instead of postponing action.

3. If a brief reply is possible, write it on the incoming letter or memo, use a photocopy for the file, and return the original to the sender.

4. If possible, put your dictation on a tape, belt, or disk (see "Dictating Machines").

5. Use form letters and form paragraphs for routine correspondence.

6. Don't make frequent revisions. Perfectionism is time-consuming.

7. Get to the point.

8. If you have a long memo, make an outline before dictating.

9. Avoid unnecessary copies. They waste somebody's time to make, distribute, file, or read.

10. For internal correspondence, try "speed-letter" forms with carbons already inserted and with space for a reply.

11. Don't write when a phone call will do. Espe-

cially if there is something to be negotiated, or ideas to be exchanged, do it by phone or face to face, instead of on paper. Use memos primarily to announce, to remind, to confirm, or to clarify.

12. Use short, terse words. Don't perpetrate polysyllabic obfuscation.

CRISIS

Whenever you are faced with a crisis, ask yourself, "What can I do to prevent this crisis from recurring?"

Many of the crises that arise in business or in personal life result from failure to act until a matter becomes urgent, with a result that more time is required to do the job. For example, if you are behind schedule with an annual printing job, you can't mail your manuscript to the printer, you must hand-deliver it; you can't wait for him to deliver proofs, you must have someone pick them up; you can't delegate various tasks in connection with the job, you must do them yourself in order to gain time.

Whenever such a crisis occurs write yourself a note and put it in your "Future" file to appear on the date you should start working.

Failure to start early enough is only one cause of crises. Others include misunderstandings due to unclear communications, lack of periodic status reports that can serve as an early-warning system, failure to follow through after delegating, and failure to make contingency plans.

Analyze each crisis, and see if you can devise ways of preventing a repetition. You'll find you can save enough time and energy to enable you to deal effectively with those relatively few cases in which circumstances totally beyond your control make it necessary to push the panic button.

DEADLINES

You can greatly increase your effectiveness if you simply give yourself a deadline for each task and do your best to stick to it. Most people work better under a little pressure, and a self-imposed deadline can provide the pressure you need to keep at your task until it is completed. Until you set a deadline for a project it isn't really an action program; it is more like a vague wish, something you want to do sometime.

Remember Parkinson's Law: "Work expands to fill the time available for its completion." It follows that an assignment to yourself or others should never be open-ended.

Sometimes it helps to announce your deadline, so that other people are expecting you to have the work done by a certain time. This increases your motivation.

If the job is complex, give yourself intermediate deadlines, so that you can keep working at a steadier rate instead of having a burst of frantic activity just before the zero hour.

Respect deadlines. If you get into the habit of stretching them they lose their effectiveness, both as a motivator for you and as a spur to the people around you.

DELEGATION

The first recorded example of failure to delegate is found in the eighteenth chapter of Exodus.

Moses, having led his people out of Egypt, was so impressed with his own knowledge and authority that he insisted on ruling personally on every controversy that arose in Israel, a task that kept him busy, as the scriptures say, "from the morning unto the evening." He served as a one-man Small Claims Court, District Court, and Supreme Court, to say nothing of his purely ecclesiastical duties. His father-in-law, a wise priest named Jethro, recognized that this was poor use of a leader's time. Speaking as the original management consultant, he said, "The thing that thou doest is not good. Thou wilt surely wear away, both thou, and this people that is with thee: for this thing is too heavy for thee; thou art not able to perform it thyself alone."

We don't know what Moses replied at this point, but I suspect that if some future Dead Sea Scrolls are uncovered giving the entire conversation, it will be found that Moses responded the way most modern executives do, with something like, "Jethro, thou art absolutely right. I agree with thee one thousand percent. I know that I am wearing myself out, and I would like to delegate more if I could. But confidentially, Jethro, thou hast no idea what a bunch of knuckleheads I have to work with. Thou simply canst not get competent help these days!"

In any event, we know that Jethro recommended a two-phase approach: first, educate the people concerning the laws and ordinances; second, select capable leaders and give them full authority over all small or routine matters, thus freeing Moses to concentrate on major decisions and long-range planning. The advice is still sound. Too many managers, like Moses, enjoy the feeling of omnipotence that comes from making all the decisions. Not only is this poor management of your own time; it also stifles creativity and smothers growth in subordinates.

You don't have to be a corporation executive to delegate, either. Parents who don't delegate household chores are doing a disservice to themselves and their children. Officers of a volunteer organization owe it to themselves and the organization to spread the blessings of involvement to as many people as possible. Running a Boy Scout troop can be as time-consuming as running General Motors if you try to do everything yourself.

One caution: giving subordinates jobs that neither you nor anyone else wants to do isn't delegating, it's assigning. And although it may be necessary at times, it doesn't nourish their egos, encourage them to grow, or enable them to assume the decision-making role that can help to free more of your time. So learn to delegate the challenging and rewarding tasks.

Delegating with strings attached is self-defeating. If you ask someone to prepare a brochure, for example, don't add a lot of detailed advice about format, typeface, and illustrations. People do a better job, and take more pride in it, if they can make such choices themselves.

The key to delegation is the word *entrust*. When you delegate, you entrust the entire matter to the other person, along with sufficient authority to make necessary decisions. This is quite a different thing from saying, "Just do what I tell you to do."

DELEGATION: *A Parable*

Once upon a time there was a Little Red Hen who owned a wheat field. "Who will help me harvest the wheat?" she asked.

"Not I," said the pig. "I don't know how."

"Not I," said the cow. "I'm too clumsy."

"Not I," said the dog. "I'm busy with some other things."

So the Little Red Hen did it herself.

"Who will help me grind the wheat into flour?" she asked.

"Not I," said the pig. "That is another vocation in which I'm untrained."

"Not I," said the cow. "You could do it much more efficiently."

"Not I," said the dog. "I'd love to, but I'm involved in some matters of greater urgency. Some other time, perhaps."

So she did it herself.

"Who will help me make some bread?" asked the Little Red Hen.

"Not I," said the pig. "Nobody ever taught me how."

"Not I," said the cow. "You're more experienced and could do it in half the time."

"Not I," said the dog. "I've made some other plans for the afternoon. But I'll help you next time."

So she did it herself.

That evening, when guests arrived for her big dinner party, the Little Red Hen had nothing to serve them except bread. She had been so busy doing work that could have been done by others that she had forgotten to plan a main course, prepare a dessert, or even get out the silverware. The evening was a disaster, and she lived unhappily ever after.

MORAL: A good leader will find a way to involve others to the extent of their ability. To do the job yourself is the chicken way out.

DICTATING MACHINES

The question of whether it is more efficient to dictate to a stenographer or a machine will never be resolved to everyone's satisfaction. Some people have a mental block against dictating into a cold, impersonal microphone instead of dealing with a human being. And many stenographers, having spent many hours perfecting the difficult skills of shorthand, manifest an understandable hostility toward disks, belts, and tapes. Having dictated thousands of letters each way, I choose the machine.

The advantages of the machine are obvious: it permits you to dictate at your own speed, stopping whenever necessary and for as long as necessary to check facts, or to reorganize your thoughts, without wasting someone else's time. If a word is missed, your secretary can replay the segment, instead of interrupting you to ask you to repeat it. And you can dictate when your secretary is doing something else, or when you are alone in the office, or in a hotel room, or even in your car. (For example, William F. Buckley, Jr., who receives about 600 letters a week, most of which he answers personally, handles a considerable part of his correspondence while being driven to and from his office.)

The least efficient way of communicating is to write letters in longhand for later transcription, and no one who writes more than one letter a week can afford such time waste.* If you do not have a dictating machine and have a mental block about dictating to a stenographer, try dictating *ideas*, leaving it up to the stenographer to put them into final form, or at least draft form. Many busy people routinely use this method to handle correspondence.

One caution about dictating machines: many people tend to become too wordy when talking into them. Keep it concise.

EFFICIENCY VERSUS EFFECTIVENESS

The day of the old-fashioned "efficiency expert" is long gone. Today management consultants think in terms of effectiveness, which is a broader and more useful concept.

Efficiency concerns the best ways of doing an assigned job. Effectiveness, on the other hand, concerns

* Nevertheless, approximately 40 percent of American executives interviewed in a Daniel Howard survey use this archaic system. See "Executive Workloads—the Triumph of Trivia," *Wall Street Journal* (August 13, 1968), p. 1.

the *best use of time*—which may or may not include doing the particular job in question.

For example, suppose you have a list of people you must telephone concerning an upcoming meeting. If you were thinking in terms of efficiency, you would consider when would be the best time to call them, whether their names might be put on automatic dialing cards in order to save time, whether the list is accurate and current, and so on. But if you were thinking in terms of effectiveness you would ask yourself if calling these people is the best use of your time. You would consider alternative methods of communicating; you would examine the possibility of delegating the task to someone else, or perhaps eliminating it altogether, in order that your time could be used more effectively.

Sound time management involves thinking in terms of effectiveness first and efficiency second.

EXERCISE

If you are too busy to exercise, you are too busy.

In your hierarchy of values, nothing can have higher priority than health, and if you find time for watching television but not for tennis or golf or jogging, you are violating the most basic rule of time management, which is to do the most important things first.

Aside from the benefits of regular exercise to your lungs and heart and digestive system, there is an incidental benefit related to time management. The aggressiveness with which you perform tasks throughout the day is closely related to your physical vigor. Being in good physical condition can increase the percentage of your working hours that can be considered "prime time," during which your output is maximized.

Successful business leaders know this and use a variety of ways to keep in shape. John R. Beckett, head of San Francisco's Transamerica Corporation, finds time for a morning and evening swim every day, plus frequent skiing, fishing, hiking, and tennis-playing—and he still has time to direct the activities of a four-billion-dollar corporation. Eugene J. Sullivan, president of Borden, Inc., finds walking the ideal exercise and formed the habit of walking twenty blocks to his office every day. He lost ten pounds over a period of several months with only minimum attention to diet. In-place jogging is the method preferred by John Connor, chairman of Allied Chemical Corporation, who maintains a trim weight of 175 pounds by fifteen minutes of jogging and other exercises twice a day.

If executives who carry the responsibilities of huge industrial establishments are able to find time in their demanding schedules for exercise, surely those of us whose responsibilities are somewhat more modest should be able to schedule a half-hour a day to keep in shape!

FEAR

Procrastination wears many disguises—laziness, indifference, forgetfulness, overwork—but behind the mask, I am convinced, is usually a single emotion: fear. It may be fear of pain (as in postponing a visit to the dentist) or, more commonly, fear of embarrassment, rejection, or failure.

Analyze your fears. Precisely what are you afraid of? Is your fear real or exaggerated? Is there anything you can do to increase your chances of success—getting additional facts, rehearsing a presentation, seeking advice? Fears that have persisted for a long time in the form of vague uneasiness at a subconscious level often dissipate as soon as they are faced squarely and alternatives are honestly examined.

Above all, ask yourself, "What is the worst thing that can happen?" Often it would be only a moment's embarrassment, or the need to admit a mistake.

Sometimes, however, the fear will remain. In this case, the key words to remember are *act as if*. Try to picture yourself actually doing the thing you are postponing; "see" yourself making the sales pitch or giving the speech or confronting the hostile committee, and imagine yourself doing it coolly and with self-confidence. Then tell yourself that no matter how much fear you may feel, you are going to act as if you had none. Whether you call this process the self-fulfilling prophecy, or psychocybernetics, or psyching yourself, or merely positive thinking, the fact remains, as millions of people have found, that it works!

FILES, PROLIFERATION OF

When the English merchandising firm of Marks & Spencer began its famous war on paper work (see page 70) it discovered that it was able to abolish two-thirds of its files. After the system had been in effect ten years, a key corporate executive said, "I can only remember two instances when we couldn't find what we wanted." A small price to pay for the elimination of tons of files!

The reason files get out of hand is that we ask ourselves the wrong question when deciding whether or not to file something. We ask, "Is it conceivable that I might want to refer to this again someday?" The answer is always yes (anything is "conceivable"), so we file everything.

Instead of asking that question, use this one: "If I wanted this item again someday and didn't have it, what would I do?" Usually you would get along just fine without it. But if it were really needed, there are usually simple ways of getting it. For example, why maintain a file of the company's employee publications when you know that if you needed a back issue you could get it by calling the publication office? Why file an announcement from the personnel office that next Monday will be a holiday? Note it on your calendar, then throw away the memo. In the unlikely event that some question arises, you know that a copy is on file in the personnel office, and the worst that could happen would be that you'd have to phone a clerk there for another copy or for the information you need.

Excessive record-keeping is a symptom of insecurity and defensive thinking. It indicates that you are less concerned with attaining objectives than you are with documentation, and that your thinking is oriented to the past, not the present. Unless you happen to be in the library business, your organization's goals probably have nothing to do with the accumulation of records, so always follow the Marks & Spencer maxim, "If in doubt, throw it out!"

FILES, TWO THOUGHTS ON

1. The general rule is: A few fat files are better than a lot of thin ones.

It may appear more efficient to have file categories

with numerous subdivisions, but the more subdivisions you have the more chance there is for misfile because of somebody's misinterpretation of the primary subject matter.* Sure, it takes a bit longer to go through a fat file to find what you want, but you save more than enough time in filing (and avoidance of errors) to make up for it.

Within reason, of course.

2. Files should be the exclusive domain of whoever does the filing. Bosses should keep their cotton-pickin' hands out of the filing cabinets and should refrain from requiring that specific categories be set up, because the minds of bosses and file clerks seldom run in the same channels. (Remember what we said about delegation?)

FOLLOW-UP

If you ask people to do things and they usually don't get around to them, stop asking yourself, "What's the matter with people these days?" Instead, ask your-

---

* One recent estimate put the average cost of a misfile at $61.23.

self, "What's the matter with *me*? What am I doing (or failing to do) that causes people to give me empty promises?"

Chances are you have been training them to do just that. Whenever you ask someone to do something, whether that person is a subordinate, a co-worker, a friend, or, yes, even your boss, that person generally asks himself or herself what the chances are that the task can be "forgotten"—*based on past experience with you*. If you have established a pattern of invariably following through on assignments, your project is going to get priority treatment. Nobody enjoys having to make excuses. But if there's a pretty good chance, based on past experience, that you won't follow through, your project is likely to wind up on the back burner, maybe permanently.

One way of reminding yourself to follow through, and of gently convincing the other person that you intend to, is to use some kind of form, such as that on the next page, to keep track of assignments and deadlines. Have such a form at hand whenever you attend a meeting; it's an easy way to keep track of what was decided and to avoid misunderstandings about assigned responsibilities. Some supervisors find it useful to post such a list on a unit bulletin board. But in most cases the mere knowledge that such a list exists, and that it will be the basis of follow-up action, is sufficient to keep things moving.

Remember, though, that following through on requests is only one part of the process. Behavior-modification experts emphasize that the most important element in a training situation is what happens when the task is done right, not wrong. So when associates

Assignment Sheet

Date Assigned	Person Responsible	Action	Due Date	Completed

Relying on an assignment record such as this instead of depending on memory greatly increases chances that tasks you delegate will be performed on time.

complete an action before the deadline, mention to them that you appreciate their timely response. The behaviorists call this positive reinforcement. The transactional analysis psychologists call it stroking. Others call it common courtesy. Whatever you call it, it works wonders.

While some follow-up is essential in any organization, if you find yourself spending too much time checking up on people something is wrong. In that case, ask yourself these questions:

1. Am I making myself clear? Do I ask for specific actions, or do I phrase requests in ambiguous terms, such as, "I'd appreciate it if sometime you would . . ." or "It might be a good idea to . . ."

2. Do I set a deadline (or better still, get a mutually agreed-upon deadline) whenever I make an assignment?

3. Do I confirm important requests in writing?

4. Do my subordinates understand that I prefer that they initiate status reports, so that routine follow-through is unnecessary?

5. Do I encourage others to speak up when they question the value of an assignment instead of "forgetting" tasks that they consider unimportant?

FUN

Time management and fun go hand in hand. Work is fun only when you have it under control, when you know what your objective is, and when you are moving toward that objective. And leisure is fun only when you can relax without feeling guilty, knowing that you've earned a good rest.

So if you have negative thoughts about managing your time, forget them. Put into practice the principles of this book, and you'll not only get more done, but you'll get a lot more out of life.

GOALS

If you want to manage your time better, the first step, as suggested by time management consultant Alan Lakein*, is to ask yourself this question: *"Exactly what are my goals?"*

Take a blank sheet of paper. List your personal

* Alan Lakein, *How to Get Control of Your Time and Your Life* (New York: Peter H. Wyden, Inc., 1973).

lifetime goals, the things you would like to be able to look back upon by the time you are eighty. Not general things, such as to be happy, but specific goals such as a trip to Europe, a master's degree, a savings-account balance of a specific figure, a vacation home, a specific weight loss, a working knowledge of Spanish, and so on.

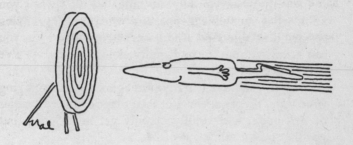

Now list your professional goals. Not such generalities as a higher salary or a promotion or greater prestige, but specific things like a salary of a certain amount, promotion to a particular job, or election to a specific office in a professional society.

Then make a list of short-term goals, the things you would like to accomplish in the next six months.

Besides being specific, goals should be attainable and authentic—in other words, *things you really want and are willing to work for*. Keep in mind that they are subject to change at any time; indeed, one of your priority tasks should be to look over your list of goals and update it. But the list should represent your best judgment of what you'd like to accomplish as of this moment.

Now, analyze your lists. They probably include

more things than you reasonably can expect to do, so assign priorities. Select the three or four goals in each category that you consider most important and write them down some place where you will see them every day. Memorize them. And a hundred times a day, ask yourself, *"Is what I am doing now moving me closer to one of my goals?"* If the answer is no, figure out some way the activity can be eliminated, delegated to someone else, or downgraded in priority so that it can be accomplished in your least productive time.

IF ONLY

There is no greater waste of time than regret.

A famous New York psychiatrist, nearing the end of a long and illustrious career several years ago, said that the most useful concept he had discovered for helping people turn their lives around was what he called his "four little words." The first two were *if only*. "Many of my patients have spent their lives living in the past," he said, "anguishing about what they should have done in various situations. 'If only I had prepared better for that interview . . .' 'If only I had expressed my true feelings to the boss . . .' 'If only I had taken that accounting course . . .' "

Wallowing in this sea of regret is a serious emotional drain. The antidote is simple: eliminate those two words from your vocabulary. Substitute the words *next time*, and tell yourself, "Next time I'm going to be prepared . . . Next time I'm going to speak out . . . Next time I have a chance I'm going to take that class . . ."

Practice this simple technique until it becomes a habit. Never rehash errors you've made. When you find yourself doing so, simply tell yourself, "Next time I'll do it differently." You'll find this closes the door on the matter, freeing you to devote your time and your thoughts to the present and the future instead of the past.

INDECISION

If you are the kind of person who vacillates agonizingly between two courses of action, even on minor matters, fearful that whichever course you choose might turn out to be a mistake, keep this in mind: *in-*

decision is nearly always the worst mistake you can make. If you choose the alternative that seems better and announce it confidently and proceed full speed ahead, you will usually make out better than if you agonize for a long time over a difficult choice.

Some decisions, such as whether to change jobs, obviously require a great deal of thought and should not be made hastily. But once the available facts are in hand, the effective individual will reach a decision and then stop mentally churning the pros and cons, so that he can devote his full efforts to making the decision work.

As for minor decisions—the day-to-day garden variety decisions that we all have to make—generally the more quickly the decision is made, the better. If you postpone action until *all* objections are overcome, you will never get anything done.

INFORMATION OVERLOAD

The office duplicating machine, the mimeograph, the offset press, the videotape recorder—all these and many more products of modern technology have one common goal: the production and distribution of more and more information to be absorbed by the human brain. But no one has come up with any ideas for increasing the human brain's capacity to absorb more information.

And yet, as sociologist-economist Kenneth E. Boulding has pointed out, "the crucial element in social systems is not information but knowledge. All a computer does is process information. Knowledge, on the other hand, is obtained much more by the loss of information than by the gain of it. In fact, that's what an organization is all about. Somebody has called an organization a hierarchy of wastebaskets. In other words, a structure to prevent information from reaching the executive desk. Otherwise, the executive gets an information overload."*

This is one of the arguments against speed-reading courses. Even assuming that they do what they claim to do, most people are already taking in more information than they can usefully assimilate. Why multiply the input, especially the input of the kind of material that can be read at several thousand words per minute?

You can cope with the deluge of printed material and junk mail that comes in simply by having your secretary screen out everything that is obviously worthless or by liberal use of the wastebasket as you open your mail. Cancel subscriptions that don't give you enough value for the time you spend reading them. The internal company communications that come across your desk, however, are sometimes more difficult to deal with.

* Quoted in Robert W. Glasgow, "Aristocrats Have Always Been Bitches," *Psychology Today* (January 1973), p. 63.

The two most common reasons for excessive internal communication are the following:

1. *Failure to delegate completely*. If subordinates feel that they don't have the authority to handle problems, they invariably pass the buck to their superior, providing detailed input and then waiting for the decision to be made for them (see "Upward Delegation").

2. *Management by procedures rather than by objectives*. When people are judged by how well they comply with directives, rather than by how well they meet the organization's objectives, paper work will multiply: a proliferation of memos and reports designed to prove that procedures are being followed.

Make it clear to your subordinates that you expect to be kept informed about progress toward objectives and about problems requiring your attention. But make it equally clear that you do not want to be bothered by submission of quantities of routine information that will make it difficult for you to concentrate on the big picture.

INTERRUPTIONS

You can't eliminate interruptions. Most of those interruptions, in fact, are simply requests that you do whatever it is that you get paid for doing. Talking to a customer, answering an employee's question, responding to a call from your boss—these are what your job is all about.

Still, you can minimize the number of interruptions, and you must if you're going to operate effectively, because one hour of concentrated effort is worth more than two hours of ten- or fifteen-minute segments. It takes time to warm up your mental motor after an interruption, especially if you return to the project hours or days later.

So, some suggestions:

1. *Analyze your incoming phone calls, preferably after logging them for several days.* Are you frequently getting calls that have to be referred to other people, or that are simply unnecessary? Determine what could be done to cut down on them.

For example, a switchboard operator might not know what questions to ask of a caller to make sure the call is referred to the right person. Or perhaps the company's internal telephone directory contains misleading job titles, or lists departments in such a way that it is not clear exacly what each department does. Or maybe the directory is not current. These seem to be trifling details, but if they contribute to a pattern of misdirected calls they should be identified and dealt with.

A more basic cause of unnecessary interruptions, however, is lack of an effective system of communication. If people aren't informed when the new price list will be published, or what the holiday schedule will be, or why certain payroll deductions were made, they must interrupt someone, either by phone or in person, to find out.

2. *Use a call-back system for phone calls*. Some people are important enough to be put through any time, but for other calls that don't appear to be emergencies, have your secretary get the name and number so that you can call back at your own convenience. If you answer your own phone, a quick "I'll call you back at 11:30" will minimize the interruption. By bunching your calls during a period before lunch or toward the end of the day, when people are less inclined to chat, you can handle calls much more efficiently.

Many people prefer to answer their own phone and to take calls as they come, to demonstrate their accessibility. If this policy fits in with your operating style, fine. But most people will find that the call-back system saves time in the long run.

3. *Set the tone of the conversation at the beginning*. It's possible to answer the phone in a cordial manner, followed by an inquiry such as "What can I do for you?" indicating that while you want to be friendly, you also want to be businesslike. On the other hand, if you simply indulge in pleasantries such as, "It's sure good to hear from you again, how are things going?" and so on, you signal that you have time to kill, and the conversation is likely to take many minutes

longer. The same principle applies, of course, to personal visits.

4. *Set aside a time for phone calls and consultations.* It can be very helpful in an office if people let it be known what times they are available and what times they prefer not to be disturbed. Co-workers understand the need for this kind of arrangement and will not take offense if you explain in advance that you prefer to see people and handle phone calls, for example, before 9:30 and after 11:30, and before 3:00 and after 4:30, thus leaving a substantial block of time in both morning and afternoon to concentrate on major projects. You explain, of course, that this is merely a guideline and that urgent matters should be brought to your attention immediately.

5. If you have the kind of job that permits it, consider the possibility of spending an occasional morning or even a full day working at home, where interruptions are less likely.

6. If most of your interruptions come from your boss, don't assume that you must put up with them. Pick a judicious time (probably not when an interruption has just occurred!) to explain that you are trying to get better control of your time, and ask if you could arrange mutually convenient times each day to check with each other on routine matters. Chances are your boss will appreciate your interest in operating more effectively and may even get the message that everyone, even the boss, needs to give some thought to time-management practices.

LISTS

I recommend keeping two lists for each day—preferably on the same sheet of paper.

On one side of the sheet (or in your appointment book) list those items scheduled for a specific time, such as meetings and appointments. On the other side, put your "To Do" list, a random listing of everything you would like to accomplish during the day. Then look over your "To Do" list and number everything in order of priority. Probably most of the value of the list is in accomplishing the items marked number one and num-

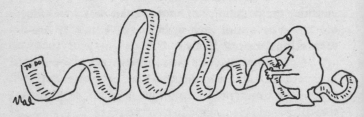

ber two (see "Pareto Principle"), so schedule a specific block of time to work on those items. Plan to do the others, in order of priority, as time permits. Don't schedule secondary tasks for specific times; you need to maintain enough flexibility to handle unexpected interruptions. Otherwise, your plan will be impractical and you will become discouraged.

One serious limitation of a "To Do" list is that it is usually compiled on the basis of urgency. It includes things that demand immediate attention, some of which are important and some of which are not; but *it usually does not include the things that are important but not urgent*, such as long-range planning and major projects that you want to accomplish but that nobody is pushing you to do.

So always, when making up your daily list of things that need to be done, take a moment to review your list of objectives (see "Goals") and see if the things you are working on are really the things that will get you closer to where you want to be.

Chances are you won't get to the bottom of your "To Do" list by the end of the day, but don't let that worry you. If you've worked according to priorities you've accomplished the important things, and that's what time management is all about.

One word of caution, however: when you find yourself transferring an item from today's list to tomorrow's list more than once or twice, it may be that it is a low-priority item, but it also may be that you are procrastinating. In that case, instead of holding it over again, admit to yourself that you're goofing off, and figure out what to do about it (see "Procrastination").

I strongly recommend spending the last few minutes of each working day preparing your list for the next morning. In talking with successful executives about time-management practices, I have found this mentioned more frequently than anything else as an aid to effective planning. If delayed until morning, list preparation is often done haphazardly because of the press of other activities, and the list tends to be made up of only the urgent matters, rather than the important ones.

LUNCH HOUR

The "business" lunch is a time trap. It is based on the theory that if you break bread with someone, you have the inside track to that person's pocketbook, ideas, or affection, whichever it is you're after.

The theory has some validity, and meeting someone for lunch can be a way of using time effectively. Too often, however, it is counterproductive. It tends to run to two hours, including travel time. It usually involves eating more heavily than usual (including perhaps a martini or two), contributing to midafternoon torpor. And it usually involves doing in two hours what could be accomplished in twenty minutes.

A far better use of time usually is a light lunch and a brisk walk. Even a brief nap, if you can be so lucky.

A practice that many people find useful is to postpone lunch until 1 P.M. or later, using the noon hour for work. In most offices, phone calls and other interruptions are less likely then—and you have the added bonus of quicker service at the cafeteria or in a restaurant when the rush hour is over.

MANAGEMENT BY OBJECTIVES

The noted economist and management consultant Peter Drucker coined the term Management by Objectives* in 1955. Since then the term has become part of the vocabulary of business leaders throughout the world, and in 1973 Roy Ash, then director of the Office of Management and Budget, began introducing the concept to the federal bureaucracy. In the civil service and in some large companies progress has been slow, especially at the lower levels, because MBO threatens the three basic underpinnings of a bureaucracy: tradition, centralized control, and red tape.

MBO means thinking in terms of specific goals rather than in terms of procedures and regulations. It encourages the asking of such questions as, "Exactly what are we trying to accomplish?" and, "Why should we be doing this?" and, "Is there a better way?" instead of such questions as, "Is this in keeping with agency policy?" or, "Is this what we were told to do?" or, "Will this enable our division to hire more people and have more power?"

Setting specific goals and allocating time to those activities which contibute most toward their realization are the keys to effectiveness in any organization, large

* Peter F. Drucker, *The Practice of Management* (London: Wm. Heinemann Ltd., 1955), p. 150.

or small. To use Laurence J. Peter's explanation: "Lacking an adequate objective, a typical management response is to increase input—hire more people, upgrade qualifications, urge employees to work harder. Lacking an objective that defines what the process must do, individuals may increase input and become busily engaged in useless motions producing enormous activity to accomplish nothing."*

Individuals as well as organizations easily become preoccupied with process. The salesman who faithfully makes calls on old customers long after their accounts have ceased to be productive; the teacher who grades a paper on its neatness instead of its content; the supervisor who judges subordinates by how few waves they make rather than by how many ideas they have; and the administrator who requires voluminous written reports on a project instead of checking personally to find out how it's going are some of the people who squander their own time and that of others because they have lost sight of ultimate objectives. Instead they are thinking in terms of keeping people busy, maintaining a system, and putting up a good front.

According to Roy Ash, "Management by Objectives isn't a bunch of reports, it isn't a set series of meetings, it's a new style, not a new process."†

It's the style used by those who want to get maximum results from the time they invest.

---

* Laurence J. Peter, *The Peter Prescription* (New York: Bantam Books, 1972), p. 145.
† Quoted in Joel Havemann, "OMB Begins Major Program to Identify and Attain Presidential Goals," *National Journal* (June 2, 1973), p. 783.

MEETINGS

There is no greater time-waster than poorly planned, poorly managed meetings. If you are in a position to call meetings, keep that in mind. Ask yourself: Is this meeting a substitute for action? Can I make the decision myself without involving others? Then why not do so?

If you do have to involve others, consider doing it by telephone, perhaps by conference call. Don't meet unless you need to, because every minute wasted is multiplied by the number of people in attendance.

But assume the meeting *is* needed. First, invite people *in writing*, being specific about what you hope to *decide*, not just listing subjects you want to consider.

For example, if you invite several people to your office to "discuss" product lines, you are, in effect, asking them to come and chat. Consider, instead, the effect of a memo like this:

To: F. Jones, R. Brown, J. Roberts, M. Johnson
Subject: Product lines

I would like to have you or your representative attend a one-hour meeting in my office Tuesday at 3 P.M. to decide the following regarding product lines:

1. Is our product mix becoming too complex for efficient manufacturing and marketing?
2. Would significant economies result from decreasing the number of package sizes?
3. Would the market accept this?
4. If we cut product lines or sizes, which ones should be first?

Those receiving such a memo will come to the meeting knowing exactly what information is expected and are likely to have done some thinking and some homework.

Start your meeting on time, stick with the agenda, and *try to reach some kind of decision on each item*, or assign responsibility for further action. Don't let the meeting drag on beyond the scheduled time.

But probably the most important point to remember is to restate, at the end of the meeting, the decisions reached and the assignments made. Too many meetings end with people unsure of exactly what was decided and who is supposed to do what by what date.

After the meeting—the same day, if possible— send a memo to the participants confirming what was decided, what responsibilities were assigned, and what deadlines were set for further action. Never omit this step. It clinches the assignments and establishes responsibility. And the mere act of writing such a memo will make you face up to the question of whether or not you accomplished your objectives.

So much for meetings you call. What about the meetings where someone else, such as your boss, is in charge and is wasting everyone's time by violating the suggestions outlined above?

Well, don't just sit there and let your time be wasted without trying to do something about it. If your boss doesn't prepare agendas before a meeting, suggest that this might be a good idea, "in order to keep us from getting off the track." If meetings drag on forever, suggest privately that they be scheduled for 11:30 or 4:30 "to keep the more talkative people from getting carried away." If your boss won't crystallize a decision on one subject before moving to another, volunteer to keep minutes of the meeting. This gives you a reason to interrupt and say, "Just a minute—before we go on to another subject I want to make sure my notes are accurate: what have we decided to do about the item we've been talking about?"

The reason you were invited to the meeting was because you supposedly could contribute something. Frequently the greatest contribution you can make is to help a weak chairman keep the meeting on track. So don't just sit there. Speak up!

MEMORANDA

When the mail is disposed of we have what is known as Memorandum Hour. During this period everyone sends memoranda to everyone else. If you happen to have nothing in particular about which to dictate a memorandum, you dictate a memorandum to someone, saying that you have nothing to suggest or report. This gives a stimulating exchange of ideas, and also helps to use up the blue memorandum blanks which have been printed at some expense for just that purpose.

—Robert Benchley,*
From Nine to Five

* Robert Benchley, *The Benchley Roundup* (New York: Harper & Row, 1954), p. 28.

Memo-writing can be a vicious time-waster. Aside from the time it takes to dictate, type, edit, retype, transmit, read, answer, and file a memo, there is another peril: it often encourages procrastination. By writing a memo saying that you are in the process of performing a certain task, you con yourself into believing that things are moving, that you have done something. There is then less pressure to get on with the job, now that you've gained some breathing time. But pressure is what you need, right?

Another thing to remember is that written communication tends to be one-way. Unless the other person responds in writing you don't get the feedback you need—the reactions, questions, suggestions, and arguments that ensure that your ideas are understood and are sound.

Remember, too, that people are less candid in writing than in discussion. There is a permanence about the written word that encourages caution and restraint. If you want a frank appraisal of someone's work, for example, you would be foolish to ask for a memo, or even to rely too heavily on a written personnel report. A more honest evaluation will always be obtained through a phone call.

And think of the time you save!

So avoid using the memo to carry on dialogue, to negotiate, to determine consensus. It generally should be used only to announce, to confirm, to clarify, to remind.

MENTAL BLOCKS

When you keep trying to get a job done, and nothing happens, stop. Instead of investing more time in a futile effort, analyze the problem and see if you can come up with a new approach. Usually your frustration will be caused by one of the following:

1. *Lack of facts.* If you aren't sure you have all the facts, you naturally hesitate to write that report, prepare that speech, or plan that campaign. Do some more research and see if it doesn't get you off dead center.

2. *Lack of conviction.* Maybe you are finding it impossible to get started because deep down you don't believe in the value of the task or the way in which you've been told to do it. Instead of letting this uneasiness gnaw away at you, face the facts squarely,

analyze the pros and cons, and confront your boss with a recommendation for a different course of action. If you lose, and it's a minor matter, get it done as quickly as possible so you can forget it. If it's a major matter, and part of a recurring pattern, better try to find another boss.

3. *Lack of a starting point.*   Maybe the task is so overwhelming that you can't figure out how to get started. Use the "salami technique" (see "Procrastination").

4. *Tunnel vision.*   Perhaps you are so close to the problem that you can't get a good perspective on it. Get some input from other people. Whether they have any good ideas or not, merely explaining the situation to them often will clarify your own thinking and may stimulate you to find the way out yourself.

5. *Fatigue.*   Creative thinking cannot be forced. If you are working on a problem and are getting nowhere, your best bet often is to put it on the back burner overnight and let your subconscious mind take over. Sometimes the answer will come when you least expect it—even in the middle of the night. (The late Henry Kaiser made it a practice to "assign" his subconscious mind a problem to work on just before going to sleep. He found that the answer often came to him at around 3 A.M. So he always kept a pencil and piece of paper on the nightstand to scribble a word or two, so that he could go back to sleep without worrying about forgetting.)

NAPS

There is nothing sacred about the pattern of sleeping eight hours and remaining awake for all of the remaining sixteen. The twenty-four-hour day is simply an accident of astronomy, and most animals have sense enough to take a nap whenever they feel like it, day or night.

Einstein made a nap part of his daily routine. So did Edison and Churchill. Presidents of the United States who have found naps useful in helping them to cope with the pressures of office include Presidents Truman, Eisenhower, Kennedy, and Johnson.

Not everyone has the freedom to work out such a schedule. But if you do, or even if you can stretch your lunch hour to an hour and a half or two hours by coming to the office earlier, experiment and see if your optimum working cycle might involve a midday nap.

The physical arrangements are admittedly a problem for most people. You need quiet and seclusion. If you can't go home for a nap, a nearby YMCA or private club may be the answer. Even driving to a nearby park and taking a short nap in the car provides a worthwhile break for some people.

A siesta isn't for everyone, but if you're one of those who perk up after one, do your darnedest to arrange your schedule accordingly.

NO

Of all the time-saving techniques ever developed, perhaps the most effective is the frequent use of the word *no*.

You cannot protect your priorities unless you learn to decline, tactfully but firmly, every request that does not contribute to the achievement of your goals.

The tendency of many time-pressured people is to accept grudgingly new assignments in volunteer organizations, new social obligations, new chores at the office, without realistically weighing the cost in time. Such people worry about offending others—and wind up living their lives according to other people's priorities.

At work, of course, you cannot always turn down the request that you take on a job that you think a waste of time. But you can win a good percentage of the time if you try. Point out to your boss how the new task will conflict with higher-priority ones and suggest alternatives. If your boss realizes that your motivation is not to get out of work but to protect your time to do a better job on the really important things, you'll have a good chance of avoiding unproductive tasks. But you have to speak up.

OFFICE ARRANGEMENT

Obsession with office furnishings is often a sign of what Laurence Peter calls the "final placement syndrome," evidence that one is losing sight of objectives and beginning to concentrate on status and appearances.* Still, environment has a bearing on effectiveness, and attention must be given to those elements that affect time use.

For executives, a common problem is an arrangement where it is difficult or impossible for a secretary to screen visitors effectively. The open-door policy of modern business has advantages, but unless there are restraints it can be abused. If it isn't possible to get greater privacy by closing a door (an option that is, of course, unavailable to most office workers), often the same end can be accomplished by repositioning the

* Laurence J. Peter, *The Peter Prescription* (New York: Bantam Books, 1972).

desk, so that it isn't so close to the stream of traffic, or so that one's back is turned to those who most frequently interrupt.

As Alec Mackenzie points out, "Physical propinquity is a very real factor in determining the frequency of communication."* If you have inadequate personal communication with certain co-workers, consider the possibility of getting your desk located closer to theirs. If, on the other hand, you find certain people are wasting your time, coming to you with problems that they could handle as easily by themselves, consider changing the physical arrangement so that you are not as accessible.

The desk itself can be a factor in effective time use. One system that many people find useful is to have a two-level arrangement—a regular desk at which they can sit, and an adjacent area at which they can work standing up. For example, John R. Beckett, head of Transamerica Corporation, has a stand-up desk that pops out from behind a panel in his office, and he finds he spends more time using that than his regular desk. Writers Thomas Wolfe and Ernest Hemingway found that they were able to write better standing up. Fletcher L. Byrom, chairman of Koppers Corporation, has a high desk, especially designed for him, at which he does most of his work. When he wants to sit down he uses a high stool. For a full-time office worker, the dual arrangement has the obvious advantage of providing an opportunity to switch back and forth from a standing to a sitting position to relieve tedium and fatigue, thereby increasing the supply of "prime time."

* R. Alec Mackenzie, *The Time Trap* (New York, AMACOM, 1972), p. 63.

The deskless office is an innovation some executives use to conserve time. One advocate of this is Lawrence A. Appley, former chairman of the board of the American Management Association, who insists that "most desks only bury decisions." He believes that those executives who are high enough in the organization to work primarily through other people are likely to be more effective if they have no desk on which papers can accumulate. For top management of large corporations this arrangement may be worth considering, but for most people a desk is a necessity, and there are other ways of keeping paper work moving.

Office arrangement does affect time use and is worth careful analysis. Plan for a certain amount of privacy (but not so much that you become inaccessible) and try to arrange your physical surroundings so that you can do the job at hand with a minimum of distraction or fatigue.

OVERSTAFFING

"Many hands make light work," my mother used to say when she wanted help with the dishes. But in an office it ain't necessarily so. Many hands make work, period.

Suppose you are a conscientious worker in an office where there isn't enough important work to keep everybody busy. What do you do? Because you want to feel useful, you begin looking for tasks that might have at least some marginal value. You could arrange a survey, prepare a questionnaire, update the policy manual, reorganize the filing system, change the standard personnel forms, generate some red tape, set up a committee, call a meeting, anything to hide from yourself and others the fact that you are not busy on something important.

Or, if you can't find something constructive to do, you might simply undertake a vendetta against some other department or person. After all, if you're in a nonessential slot you are vulnerable, and you'd better get your licks in first.

All of this turbulence and make-work is a result of having too many people in the organization. In a lean organization people are too busy for trivia, so they don't have these problems.

Well, not to the same extent, anyway.

PAPER WORK, COST OF

People who can't understand the importance of simplifying procedures in order to save time can sometimes see the picture better when it is put in terms of saving money.

Suppose that you are running a small business and must hire one additional clerk, at a salary of $100 per week, to cope with unnecessary record-keeping, filing, correspondence, and other paper work. Suppose that you operate at a profit of 5 percent of sales. That means that you must sell an additional $104,000 worth of merchandise just to pay the salary of that clerk—and that doesn't include fringe benefits.

To put it another way, remember that every reduction in cost is a 100 percent addition to net profit. And elimination of time-consuming reports, filing procedures, excessive written communications and other unnecessary paper work is a good place to start. Too often cost-cutting efforts are limited to such obvious targets as new equipment, advertising budget, travel, and turning out the lights, and too little attention is paid to ways of saving money by saving time.

"Time is money," according to the old maxim. You'd better believe it.

PAPER WORK: THE MARKS & SPENCER EXPERIENCE

In 1956, Sir Simon Marks, multimillionaire chairman of Marks & Spencer, Britain's most prosperous retail chain, noticed the lights burning in one of his retail stores long after closing. He discovered that two employees were working overtime on stock cards. He investigated and learned that nearly a million such cards were filled out each year and sent to London to keep track of inventory. He ordered a study to determine

whether the cards were really necessary. It turned out that they were not; a simpler way of keeping inventory was developed, involving spot checks and (horror of horrors!) even going so far as to let the stockroom clerk look at the shelves and simply reorder when supplies of certain items were getting low.

The success of this effort caused the company to

launch the most massive war on paper work Britain had ever seen. Every form used by the company, every file, every paper-work-creating procedure was scrutinized, and the staff was told to ask, "Would our entire business collapse if we dispensed with this?" The motto was "If in doubt, throw it out."

Within a year, 26 million cards and sheets of paper, weighing 120 tons, had been eliminated. Time cards, for example, were abolished, a million of them a year. Supervisors were trusted to know who was putting in a good day's work and who wasn't.

The Marks & Spencer campaign was no flash in the pan. Effective use of time through simplification and elimination of paper work has been the guiding principle of the firm ever since, and it has worked. Between 1956 and 1973 sales increased 361 percent, profits increased 600 percent, and store area was doubled. Yet the staff decreased during that period from 26,700 to 26,600. Paper-work savings, and the increase in morale attributable to the paper-work decrease, is given much of the credit for that record.

Essential to the Marks & Spencer type of operation is a realization that people can be trusted, that managers will manage better if given freedom within general guidelines instead of being required through reports and manuals to comply with detailed instructions. Another cornerstone of the philosophy is the idea of "sensible approximation," which means that getting figures close enough for all practical purposes is more efficient than striving after perfection for its own sake.

Companies in the United States and elsewhere have studied and profited by the Marks & Spencer experience. CBS, for example, undertook a thorough housecleaning of its record-keeping system several years ago and was able to eliminate 15 million pieces of filed paper. One major oil company managed to eliminate two-fifths of its records and cut expenditures for new file cabinets from $20,000 to $5,000 a year.

Examine the paper work in your own office and see if every report, every multiple copy, every questionnaire, every file, really justifies the time and energy it requires. Then apply Sir Simon's rule: if in doubt, throw it out!

PAPER-WORK QUIZ

The old saying "A place for everything, and everything in its place" applies particularly to paper work, because having a well-established routine makes it possible to concentrate on the content of the message instead of worrying about how you will keep track of it.

The purpose of this quiz is not to help you come up with a right answer, because there are no *right* answers. One person might give a certain paper to a secretary, another might put it in a desk file, and both are "right" if they act out of habit, having set up a system, instead of having to agonize over the decision.

So answer these questions quickly, indicating not what you *should* do, but what you probably *would* do. If you have to think about it for a while, or if you probably would set the item aside and come back to it later, put a question mark. More than two or three question marks suggests that you need to set up a better system for handling paper work.

Where would you put this paper?

1. Bill for materials you have purchased.

_____

2. Trade journal. Appears to have articles worth reading, but you don't have time to read them now.

_____

3. Memo from your boss asking you to attend a meeting next Monday.

_____

4. Questionnaire from a business school asking your opinion on personnel practices.

_____

5. Material from a subordinate that you will use in preparing your next monthly report of activities.

_____

6. Letter requiring a prompt answer, but you are going to have to make some phone calls before you can answer it.

_____

7. Form letter from a person you call frequently, giving new address and phone number.

_____

8. Memo from another division of your organization, asking for copies of a report prepared by your department. _____

9. Brochure from a company selling business forms. You think some of the forms may be worth ordering, but you are not sure. _____

10. Letter of complaint from a customer. _____

11. Memo from personnel department concerning procedure for personnel evaluation. _____

12. Note you have written to yourself as a reminder to start sooner next year on budget preparation. _____

Although there are no *right* answers to the questions in the foregoing quiz, some discussion is in order, because there are some *wrong* answers that clearly violate principles of effective time use:

1. If you don't have a firm routine for handling bills, you really have problems (and so do your creditors). The main thing is to get the bill off your desk by paying it, or by bucking it to someone else for prompt payment, or by getting it into a "Future" file for payment at a later date.

2. Whatever you do, don't leave the magazine sitting on your desk where it will tempt you away from higher-priority tasks. Have a separate place, on a side table or in a drawer, for reading material.

3. If this memo lists only the time and date of the meeting, the information should be noted on your desk calendar (or pocket calendar) and the memo should be thrown away. Otherwise it clutters up files and wastes filing time. On the other hand, if it includes a detailed agenda, or is attached to material to be discussed, you will want to take it to the meeting, in which case it should go into your "Future" ("Tickler") file.

4. Decide now (not later) whether or not you will answer the questionnaire. If not, it goes into the waste-basket. If you plan to answer it, do so immediately and place it in your "Out" basket in keeping with the principle of handling each piece of paper only once.

5. This might be put into a "Future" file for the date on which the report is to be prepared, or into a "Subject" file that will be brought out on that date. In the meantime it should be kept out of sight.

6. Leave the letter in the middle of your desk while you make those calls so that you can dictate your answer and complete the action before going on to something else. Of course, if you have to hold the letter for call-backs you should have a "Pending" file or drawer where it can be put out of sight.

7. Enter the new information in your personal phone directory and throw away the original. Or, if the information concerns others in the organization, circulate the notice to them.

8. Send the reports immediately with a buck slip (or jot a note on the original). The thing to avoid on routine matters like this is dictating a formal transmittal memo, creating additional paper work.

9. If you are not sure, drop it in the wastebasket or pass it along to someone who may be in a better

position to judge its value. Don't let it float on your desk because of indecision.

10. If you have a dictating machine, you should dictate your reply immediately. If you use a stenographer, you probably will want to place this in a pile of correspondence to be dictated at a later time. Another possibility, and one well worth considering, is to avoid a written reply and answer by phone, noting the conversation on the letter itself and then sending it to the files.

11. If it is really worth keeping, it should be placed immediately in the personnel file or given to the person who does the filing. But if it is something of a trivial or general nature, make a mental note of the contents and throw it away, keeping in mind that should you need a copy someday you could obtain one from the sender's files. In other words, "If in doubt, throw it out."

12. You should have a system that routinely will bring to your attention those things you want to consider at future times. It should be on a calendar basis rather than by subject, so that you won't have to remember to find the file. Either an accordion file with dates or dated file folders will accomplish this.

In addition to analyzing paper work in terms of whether or not a clear routine exists, it is important to analyze it in relation to the principle of delegation. For example, several of the items in the quiz clearly should be handled by a secretary or an assistant, if you have one. When going over your answers, consider whether you are the logical person to handle each item.

PARETO PRINCIPLE

The Pareto Principle, named after an Italian economist-sociologist of the late nineteenth and early twentieth centuries, states that the significant items in a given group normally constitute a relatively small portion of the total items in the group. Sometimes it is referred to as the concept of the "vital few" and the "trivial many," or the 80/20 rule.

Thus, in any sales force, about 20 percent of the salesmen usually will bring in about 80 percent of the new business. In a discussion group, 20 percent of the participants usually will make 80 percent of the comments. In a company, about 20 percent of the employees will account for about 80 percent of the absenteeism. In a classroom, 20 percent of the students will take up 80 percent of the teacher's time. This law has countless applications in every phase of living.*

The Pareto Principle can be of great help in coping with a long list of tasks to be accomplished. The mind boggles at such a list, which is often impossible to complete, and most people become discouraged before they start. Or they begin with the easiest, leaving the most difficult for the last, and never quite get around to them. It helps to know that most of the benefit to be derived from doing what is on the list probably is related to just two or three items. *Select those two or three, allo-*

---

* R. Alec Mackenzie, *The Time Trap* (New York: AMACOM, 1972), p. 51.

cate a block of time to work on each of them, and concentrate on getting them done! Don't feel guilty about not finishing the list, because if your priorities are valid most of the benefits are related to those two or three items you selected.

So whenever you are faced with the difficult task of choosing from among a number of alternatives, keep the Pareto Principle in mind. By asking yourself which items are the really significant ones, you avoid getting sidetracked on secondary activities.

PARKINSON'S LAW

Professor Parkinson was right: work expands to fill the time available for its completion.

The answer to Parkinson's Law would seem obvious: make less time available for a given task and you will get it done more quickly.

Here is where your daily time plan comes in. Without one, you will tend to dawdle at difficult tasks (or even pleasant ones) because you have no deadline. When you think in terms of the task, instead of in terms of the time available for it, the sin of perfection sets in.

You can always put one or two more finishing touches on the job, and can con yourself into chalking these up to excellence when in reality you should chalk them up to wheel-spinning.

The only way to overcome this is to work Parkinson's principle in reverse—set a deadline for each task and hold to that deadline.

PERFECTIONISM

There is a difference between striving for excellence and striving for perfection. The first is attainable, gratifying, and healthy. The second is unattainable, frustrating, and neurotic.

It's also a terrible waste of time.

Sir Simon Marks, who was chairman of the consistently profitable Marks & Spencer retailing chain in Great Britain (see page 70), maintained that those who make a fetish of perfection are wasting time and money that could be allocated better elsewhere. Hence his system of "sensible approximation" in inventory procedures. His motto: "The price of perfection is prohibitive."

A stenographer who retypes a lengthy letter because of a trivial error that could be corrected in ink, or a boss who demands that such a letter be retyped, might profit from examining the Declaration of Independence in the National Archives and noting that the inscriber of that document made two errors of omission in copying the final version. Instead of starting over, he inserted the missing letters between the lines, with the aid of a caret. If such treatment is acceptable in the case of the document that gave birth to American freedom, surely it also would be acceptable in the case of a letter that is going to be accorded a brief glance en route to someone's file cabinet or wastebasket!

PLANNING

No football coach would think of sending his team into a contest without a game plan. Such a plan is not sacred; indeed, it is almost sure to be modified as the game progresses, but it is important that there be such a plan at the outset.

You need a game plan for your day, and for your week. Otherwise you'll allocate your time according to whatever happens to land on your desk. Other people's actions will determine your priorities. And you will find yourself making the fatal mistake of dealing primarily with problems rather than opportunities.

In planning your time make a general schedule of your day, with particular emphasis on the two or three major things you would like to accomplish. One of those major things should be planning on a major project or on some task that will carry you closer to one of your lifetime goals. On Thursday or Friday do the same thing for the next week.

Remember, there is no more productive use of time than planning ahead. Studies prove what common sense tells us: the more time we spend in advance planning on a project, the less total time is required for it. Don't let today's busy work crowd planning time out of your schedule.

PRIORITIES

There are two ways of setting priorities: according to urgency or according to importance.

Most people set them according to urgency, which

is why they spend so much time putting out fires and never get started on a project until the deadline is staring them in the face.

If you set priorities according to urgency, you probably have three categories, such as:

1. Must be done today
2. Should be done today
3. Should be done sometime, but there's no hurry

Suppose you are ready to make out your income-tax return, using this system, and it's January 31. Obviously the task would not go in the first category, because you have two and a half months before it is due. It could be put in the second category, but probably won't be, because there is no urgency. Too often it will go into the third category and won't get under way until the deadline is very near. At that point you will find it difficult to find expert help and will be unable to do as thorough a job as you would like.* You mentally kick yourself and promise to start earlier next year. But you won't, because next year the same rationale will apply.

I prefer to set priorities first in terms of importance, with urgency a secondary, though significant, consideration.† This involves taking your list of things to do and examining each item first in light of the question "Does this task clearly contribute to the achievement of my lifetime goals or my short-range ob-

---

* I am assuming, of course, that you know you don't have a refund coming. People who anticipate a refund somehow select January as a good month to work on tax returns.
† Obviously, if something is both important *and* urgent it will get top priority with either system.

jectives?" If it does, put a star by it. Then number the starred items in the order in which you would like to do them, taking into account two factors: urgency and the time/benefit ratio.

The time/benefit ratio is simply a way of recognizing that even though one task may be less important than another, and may lack urgency, there may be good reason to do it first if the benefit is substantial and the amount of time involved is small. For example, your most important task of the day might be the preparation of a report, which will take most of your day. But suppose you have a couple of minor tasks you can delegate. The few minutes you take (before starting your report) to assign the tasks gives hours more lead time to those doing them. That obviously makes sense.

Another exception to the general rule of doing the more important things first is the procedure discussed under "Pareto Principle." Instead of starting your day with the most important thing on your list, you may find it better to schedule an uninterrupted block of time during the day to work on it.

After you have ranked your starred items by priority, do so with your less important items, then try to accomplish everything in order. You will have a game plan, and your day will be much more productive than if you had to stop to establish priorities each time you were ready to begin a new task.

PROCRASTINATION

If procrastination is your problem, don't put off doing something about it!

There are three ways of coping with procrastination that I have found effective: (1) the "salami technique," (2) the balance-sheet method, and (3) the systematic development of new habits.

The "Salami Technique"

A salami in its original state, before it has been cut, is unwieldy and looks unappetizing. But cut it into thin slices and it takes on quite a different aspect. Now you have something manageable, something you can "get your teeth into."

When you realize that you are procrastinating on a major task, slice it up into as many small, manageable "instant tasks" as possible. Promise yourself that you won't force yourself to get involved with the main job, provided you do at least one of the small steps on your list.

For example, suppose you have been putting off an unpleasant phone call you should make. The "salami slices" in this situation might be the following:

1. Look up the phone number and write it down.
2. Set a time to make the call. (Making it immediately calls for more willpower than you apparently

have, so let yourself off the hook in return for a firm
commitment to make it at a specific time, which you
note on your appointment calendar.)

3. Get out the file and review what's happened.
4. Decide precisely what you intend to say.
5. Place the call.

If the task happens to be a major one, the number
of "slices" may be quite large. So make a long list. The
key is to make each incremental task so simple and quick
that by itself it doesn't amount to much. If possible,
make it something that can be finished in several minutes. And then, whenever you have a few minutes to
spare between appointments or while waiting for a
phone call, knock off one of your "instant" tasks. Without such a list of items you may never get started.

Remember, the first slice—the first instant task—
is always to list *in writing* the small steps involved in
getting the job done.

"Divide and conquer" applies to tasks just as it
does to armies or enemies.

The Balance-Sheet Method

Another good way of getting yourself off dead center is to analyze, in writing, what you are doing.

On the left side of a sheet of paper make a list of
all the reasons you are procrastinating on a particular
task. On the right side list all the benefits that will ac-
crue if you go ahead and get the job done.

The effect is striking. On the left side you will
usually have only one or two pathetic excuses, such as
"It might involve an awkward confrontation" or "I

might be bored." On the other side you will find a long list of benefits, the first of which usually will be the feeling of relief that will come with getting a necessary but unpleasant task behind you.

The effect of this technique is often swift and dramatic. You awake from your lethargy and begin working to achieve the benefits you have listed.

Habit Change: A Systematic Approach

The third (and most fundamental) approach recognizes that when we fail to act as promptly as we should it usually is not because the particular task in question is extremely difficult, but rather because we have formed a habit of procrastinating whenever possible. Procrastination is seldom related to just a single item; it is usually an ingrained behavior pattern. If we can change our habits of thinking, we can make the previous two methods unnecessary.

The importance of this fact cannot be overemphasized. I am convinced that the most significant difference between effective and ineffective people is that the ineffective person habitually thinks, "This task must be done, but it is unpleasant; therefore I will put it off as long as I can," whereas the effective person habitually thinks, "This task is unpleasant, but it must be done; therefore I will do it now so I can forget about it."

But the prospect of changing a deeply rooted habit dismays many people. They've tried it many times through sheer willpower—the New Year's resolution approach—and have failed. It isn't all that difficult, though, provided you use the right system.

William James, the father of American psychology, discussed such a system in his famous essay on habit, which was published in *Popular Science* magazine in 1887, and which subsequently has been validated by the studies of behavioral scientists. As applied to changing the procrastination habit, it would work as follows:

1. Decide to start making the change immediately, as soon as you finish reading this section, while you are motivated. Taking that first step promptly is important.

2. Don't try to do too much too quickly. Instead of trying to revolutionize your entire approach, just force yourself right now to do one thing you have been putting off. Then, *beginning tomorrow morning, start each day by doing the most unpleasant thing on your "To Do" list.*

Notice that I did not say the most *important* thing on your list. The most important things should be allocated specific blocks of time (see "Pareto Principle"). The most unpleasant thing very often will be a small matter: an overdue apology you've been meaning to make; a confrontation with a fellow worker that you've been putting off; an annoying chore you know you should tackle. Whatever it is, do it before you open the mail, before you return the phone calls left over from the previous afternoon, before you begin your usual morning routine.

This simple procedure can well set the tone for your entire day. You will get a feeling of exhilaration from knowing that although the day is only fifteen minutes old, you have already accomplished the most unpleasant thing you have to do all day. After you have done this a few days you will become locked into the habit for life, because it is what the behaviorists call a self-reinforcing action—one that has an intrinsic reward that reinforces the behavior. (This is the way an infant learns to stand; the feeling of achievement the baby gets from standing reinforces the actions that were necessary to accomplish the feat the first time, and the procedure soon becomes second nature. Similarly, the "do-it-now" habit can become second nature.)

Although I have recommended that you force yourself to follow this procedure only once a day, you will find that soon it will influence decisions throughout the day. Every time you are given an unpleasant chore you will itch to get at it, so that you can get that euphoric feeling that comes from promptly disposing of a nasty task.

The beautiful thing about this system is that you don't have to do anything you weren't going to do anyway; you intended to do that chore or you wouldn't have put it on your list. It simply means making it number one on the list, instead of number five or ten.

3. There is one caution: during the period when your new habit is taking root, especially during the first couple of weeks, you must be especially careful not to permit any exceptions. William James compared it to rolling up a ball of string: a single slip can undo more than many turns can wind up. So be tough with yourself, just for the first few minutes of the day, each day for the next two weeks, and I can promise you a new habit of priceless value.

So set this aside and start. Now.

PROTECTING PRIME TIME

If you are an office worker there are far greater peaks and valleys in your achievement level than there are for manual workers. Chances are, most of your work gets done in only a portion of your working day, the time we might designate prime time.

For most people, the first couple of hours of the day are prime time. But many of us ignore this fact and spend those hours doing routine tasks: reading the morning mail (which seldom contains top-priority items), reading periodicals, glancing through the morning newspaper, making routine phone calls, and so on. It doesn't take much thought to see the waste this entails; the best time of the day should be spent on the things that matter most, the things that require top energy, complete alertness, greatest creativity.

So schedule your one or two highest-priority tasks for the day in your prime time, and work at the low-priority tasks when you can.

Now that you've chosen your priorities and scheduled them for your prime time, the next step is to get people to leave you alone long enough to get them done. (See "Interruptions.")

RADICAL SURGERY

Time-wasting activities are like cancers. They serve no useful function, they drain off vitality, they never disappear of their own accord, and they have a tendency to grow.

The only cure is radical surgery. If you are wasting time in volunteer groups that you don't believe in, or in social activities that are a bore, or in office practices that divert you from your department's real goals, face up to the fact that these things are sapping your time and energy, and do whatever needs to be done to cut them out, once and for all.

Robert Townsend suggests that every company should have a vice president in charge of killing things. He says, "General Foods, the AFL-CIO, the Bureau of the Budget, and the Ford Foundation should make it a practice to wipe out their worst product, service, or activity every so often. And I don't mean cutting it back or remodeling it—I mean right between the eyes."*

The principle applies to personal habits, routines, and activities as much as to corporate ones.

Check your time log, your appointment calendar, your extracurricular activities, your reading list, your television viewing habits, and ax everything that doesn't give you a feeling of accomplishment or satisfaction.

* Robert Townsend, *Up the Organization* (New York: Fawcett World Library, 1970), p. 75.

SELF-QUIZ

If you want to get an idea of how effectively you are managing your own time, give yourself the following quiz:

	Yes	No
1. Do I have—in writing—a clearly defined set of lifetime goals?	☐	☐
2. Do I have a similar set of goals for the next six months?	☐	☐
3. Have I done something today to move me closer to my lifetime goals? My short-term goals?	☐	☐
4. Do I have a clear idea of what I want to accomplish at work during the coming week?	☐	☐
5. Do I try to do the most important tasks during my prime time?	☐	☐
6. Do I concentrate on objectives instead of procedures, judging myself by accomplishment instead of by amount of activity?	☐	☐
7. Do I set priorities according to importance, not urgency?	☐	☐
8. Do I make constructive use of commute time?	☐	☐
9. Do I delegate as much work as possible?	☐	☐
10. Do I delegate challenging jobs as well as routine ones?	☐	☐

	Yes	No

11. Do I delegate authority along with responsibility? ☐ ☐

12. Do I prevent subordinates from delegating upward those decisions and tasks that they find difficult or worrisome? ☐ ☐

13. Do I effectively use the aid of subordinates to get better control of my time? ☐ ☐

14. Have I taken steps to prevent unneeded information and publications from reaching my desk and intruding on my time? ☐ ☐

15. When debating whether to file something, do I follow the principle "If in doubt, throw it out"? ☐ ☐

16. In meetings, do I try to crystallize what the issues are and summarize the decisions made and responsibilities assigned? ☐ ☐

17. Do I try to handle matters by phone or in person whenever I have a choice, using written communication only when it is clearly indicated? ☐ ☐

18. Do I try to put work out of my mind when away from the office, except in clear emergencies? ☐ ☐

19. Do I force myself to make minor decisions quickly? ☐ ☐

20. Am I on guard against the recurring crisis, taking steps to make sure that it won't occur again? ☐ ☐

21. Do I always set deadlines for myself and others? ☐ ☐

22. Do I force myself to take time to plan? ☐ ☐

	Yes	No

23. Have I discontinued any unprofitable routines or activities recently? ☐ ☐

24. Do I keep things in my pocket or briefcase that I can work on whenever I get spare moments: in lines, waiting rooms, trains, planes? ☐ ☐

25. Do I try to live in the present, thinking in terms of what needs to be done now instead of rehashing past errors or successes or worrying about the future? ☐ ☐

26. Do I make periodic use of a time log to determine whether I am slipping back into unproductive routines? ☐ ☐

27. Am I continually striving to establish habits that will make me more effective? ☐ ☐

28. Do I keep in mind the dollar value of my time? ☐ ☐

29. Do I apply the Pareto Principle whenever I am confronted with a number of different tasks that need to be done? ☐ ☐

30. Am I really in control of my time? Are my actions determined primarily by me, not by circumstances or by other people's priorities? ☐ ☐

Give yourself this quiz every six months. If any of your answers are no, review the appropriate section and determine what you can do to correct the deficiency. The price of effective time use is eternal vigilance and the rewards are well worth it.

SLEEP

The notion that everyone needs eight hours' sleep each night is a myth. Some people need eight, or even more, but most of us can do nicely with less.

According to Dr. Peter Hauri, director of Dartmouth Medical School's Sleep Clinic, most adults average between seven and seven and a half hours per night, but for many, six or even five hours per night is plenty. Additional sleep beyond what you need just uses up time, according to Dr. Hauri. It has no health benefit and might even be detrimental.

How do you know how much sleep you need? You can't judge by how hard it is to get up at a particular time—you may find it equally hard whether you have overslept or underslept. Dr. Hauri says, "To find out how much sleep you need you should experiment with different sleep lengths, each for one or two weeks. If you feel quite alert and capable of functioning on five hours of sleep, there is no use forcing yourself to stay in bed seven hours. If you feel groggy and have difficulties concentrating at eight hours of sleep, maybe you are one of the people who need 10 hours."

Differences in sleep requirements seem to be related to metabolic differences, to temperament, and to the amount of enjoyment derived from daytime activity, according to Dr. Robert L. Van de Castle, director of the Sleep and Dream Laboratory of the Department of Psychiatry, University of Virginia. He says, "People with dull and boring jobs will sometimes resort to greater sleep time merely to avoid confronting their tedious daily routine. Therefore, I would not urge everyone to . . . get into the same sleep schedule, but most of us can get along on much less sleep than we usually do."*

It should be noted, incidentally, that sleep needs vary within the individual from time to time; more sleep is needed during periods of unusual stress or illness.

Many successful people believe that an important factor in their success is the time they gain by taking Ben Franklin's advice to "plough deep while sluggards sleep." Billionaire John D. MacArthur, for example, sole stockholder of Bankers Life and Casualty, limits himself to just a few hours' sleep and gets up at 5 A.M. The late Aristotle Onassis believed the same habit contributed much to his success. Dr. Alton Ochsner of New Orleans' famed Ochsner Clinic finds four hours sufficient, as does Dr. Michael DeBakey, the famous heart surgeon. (Both of them, however, follow the practice of another famous four-hour sleeper, Thomas A. Edison, and take occasional catnaps of five or ten minutes during the day if they feel fatigued.) Inventor R. Buckminster Fuller once adopted a routine of a half-hour nap every three hours around the clock, for a total of four hours a day, giving up the practice after a year only because it interfered with business.

And Pope Leo XIII, we are told, lived a vigorous and productive life on only three hours per night.

Admittedly, these are exceptions. But suppose you

* "Contemporary," *The Denver Post*, April 9, 1967.

are among the 25 percent of adults who can do nicely with six hours of sleep instead of the eight you now may be getting. Saving those two hours a day, Monday through Friday, would give you an extra forty hours— one additional work week—every month!

If that's too ambitious, consider what just one hour less sleep per night would mean: six extra work weeks per year, which adds up, over a working lifetime, to more than five years. Think what you could accomplish in an extra five years!

Up and at 'em!

SPEED READING

If your problem is that you spend too much time reading, a rapid-reading course won't solve it. The solution is to read more selectively.

It is true that some people have bad reading habits, such as subvocalizing or rereading phrases unnecessarily. A reading course can help break those patterns and increase speed somewhat. But a surprising number of students who make some progress in increasing reading speed report that after a few months they slip back into their old patterns. And as for the claim that some people can read forty thousand words per minute (which is the equivalent of reading *Gone with the Wind* in twelve minutes) and still comprehend what they are reading, consider the results of a test made at a major university. A pair of speed-reading-course graduates read an article in which lines from another essay had been interspersed. They were unaware that what they were reading was nonsense, until it was pointed out by another student who had not taken the speed-reading course.

Perhaps the most succinct comment on selectivity in reading is by James McCay, who asks, "Would you like to be able to read 50,000 words a minute? There are many times when it is easy to do this if you know how. All you have to be able to do is to recognize within one minute that a 50,000-word book does not suit your purposes, and decide *not* to read it."*

It is difficult to resist the lure of reading, especially when there is something less pleasant that you should

* James McCay, *The Management of Time* (Englewood Cliffs, N.J.: Prentice-Hall, 1959), p. 142.

be doing. Keep in mind these words of the British critic F. L. Lucas: "It is mere common sense never to undertake a piece of work, or read a book, without asking, 'Is it worth the amount of life it will cost?'"

That simple question can save you more time than all the speed-reading courses ever devised.

SUBORDINATES' TIME

If you have one or more subordinates chances are they consider you an obstacle to efficient use of their time. Every list of time problems I have seen includes "interruptions by boss" or "boss-imposed busy work" or "indecision by boss." Your subordinates may be too polite or too timid to tell you so, but take my word for it, you cause time problems for the people who report to you. And because your success is linked to their output and their morale, you pay a high price for it.

A little humility can help here. Make it clear to subordinates that you understand that their work sometimes can be more urgent than yours, and that in case of conflict they should use their own good judgment, or at least discuss the situation with you instead of automatically giving top priority to any request that happens to originate from On High.

Encourage subordinates to think about time use and to level with you whenever you ask them to do things they consider wasteful or inefficient. Ask them for suggestions that will help you make better use of your own time.

Also, urge your staff to keep a time log, but not unless you have done it yourself or they will resent the implication that you consider yourself blessed with omniscience. (And, as a matter of fact, you need effective time-management techniques even more than those under you because [1] your failures or successes tend to be magnified more because of your exalted status, and [2] the higher you rise in a hierarchy, the more discretionary time you have, with correspondingly more time-use decisions to be made.)

Encourage subordinates to think in terms of "managing the boss." Let them know that you recognize the degree to which their actions can control your time, and respect their time so they will respect yours.

TEMPO

After waiting eleven months for the army to reply to her inquiry about a study of Rocky Mountain

Arsenal workers exposed to nerve gas, Congresswoman Pat Schroeder of Denver sent her "First Annual Dilatory Conduct Award" (a twelve-ounce jar of Br'er Rabbit molasses) to the army's legislative liaison office.

If your organization is in the competition for such an award, ask what you can do to step up the tempo of activity and to stimulate a little wholesome impatience.

Massachusetts management consultant Charles H. Ford notes that "the tempo of a company—the speed with which it moves, makes and implements decisions, identifies and solves problems, grasps opportunities, reacts to competitive pressures or adapts to abrupt changes in marketing patterns and business climates— is something to which most executives and corporate bodies remain blissfully indifferent."* And yet, he suggests, it is often the one factor that contributes most to corporate success, or lack of it.

Tempo is a reflection of the attitude of the person in charge. If that person is goal-oriented ("Now that we know exactly what our objective is, let's do whatever has to be done to get there"), the pace is brisk. If that person is procedure-oriented ("Let's make sure we follow directives to the letter, and don't risk any mistakes"), the pace is sluggish.

At a personal level, the same thing is true. If you are dawdling, drifting, and *working at* a task instead of *doing* it, blow the whistle on yourself and answer these questions:

1. Exactly why am I trying to do this task? Is it really worthwhile? If so—

---

* Charles H. Ford, *How to Overcome Business Frustrations* (published by *Nation's Business,* Washington, D.C., 1975), p. 14.

2. Have I set a deadline for myself? Have I resolved to meet it?

3. If my life depended upon doing the task in half the time I have allocated, what shortcuts would I take? Is there really any reason *not* to take them?

To quote Charles Ford again, "The key is controlled urgency, treating every matter as something urgent to get done and out of the way. It means less time spent on useless conversation, less waiting patiently for someone else to move before you do, more action rather than putting things aside for later (whenever that is)."

TENSION AND TIME USE

There is a common belief that tension is bad, that quiet and tranquillity are the goals for which we should strive.

Nonsense. Without tension nothing gets done. Quiet and contentment are desirable (in fact, a daily period of meditation is an excellent use of time), but there must be alternating periods of tension or you can slip into lethargy. What keeps a watch going is the tension on the mainspring.

Positive tension can take many forms: a deadline that must be met, an awareness that your work is going to be judged, a sense of competition with others. These pressures bring out the best in people, challenging them to use time as effectively as possible. Good management involves building a reasonable amount of positive tension into your relationships with subordinates, and good self-management involves finding ways to put some pressure on yourself to perform. Making a public commitment to undertake a job on which you have been procrastinating, for example, is one way of putting pressure on yourself.

There is a kind of tension that is bad, of course, the kind that produces harmful stress. Tension headaches and other ailments associated with stress are often a result of frustration growing out of poor time-management practices: failure to set priorities, failure to plan ahead, failure to concentrate on a single item at a time, failure to delegate properly, indecision, failure to schedule periods of quiet time when you can tackle top-priority jobs without interruption. If bad habits are causing you undue stress, read the appropriate entry in this book, do what it says, and relax!

TIDBITS OF TIME

When the person you were supposed to meet for lunch is late, or when your car isn't ready at the shop as promised, or when you have to stand in a slow line at the bank—don't write these moments off as lost time! Consider them instead as windfall moments you can use to do something that otherwise would have to wait.

Salesmen often find that the time spent in a reception room awaiting an interview is enough to keep up on all their paper work: writing a call report about the preceding contact, writing notes to customers and prospects, planning future calls, updating expense accounts, and so on. Anyone can find appropriate small tasks that can be done in spare moments; it's just a matter of having the necessary forms or materials on hand.

I have found it useful for many years to carry a half-dozen 3 x 5 cards in the flap inside my pocket appointment book. Whenever I get an idea, or want to make a list, or see something I want to copy, I can use one of the cards.

Don't think of tidbits of time as exclusively for routine paper work or low-priority chores. Your highest-priority projects can be worked into spare minutes. If you are dividing major jobs into small "instant tasks" as recommended in the section on "Procrastination," you can have on hand some brief but important activities to undertake.

So if your time is wasted by other people's inefficiency, remember, it's your fault, not theirs.

TIME, DOLLAR VALUE OF

People who are paid by the hour are much more aware of the value of time than are salaried workers. (If you don't believe this, try getting a psychiatrist or a plumber to take an hour off during the day to discuss some minor matter.)

So for purposes of time management, consider that you are being paid by the hour, whether you actually are or not. To find your rate, take your annual salary, in thousands of dollars, divide by two, and that is roughly your hourly pay.

For example, if you make $16,000 a year, you are getting about $8 an hour. When a co-worker prolongs a visit by fifteen minutes to exchange a bit of gossip, the dollar value of the time you lose is $2. And a coffee break that takes you from your work for a half-hour will cost 20¢ for the coffee and $4 for the time loss.

This isn't to suggest that you should give up coffee breaks or office chitchat. They have their place. But if you have in the back of your mind a specific measure of their dollar cost, you'll find it much easier to prevent their getting out of hand.

TIME FOR WHAT?

If you follow all the advice in this book, you are going to save yourself a lot of time; my guess is that you will have between one and two extra hours of discretionary time at your disposal each day. So what are you going to do with it? That's an important question, because if you're not careful, much of the time you save will get away from you before you know it, and you'll be right back where you started.

Lay claim to the time you save. Plan it. Allocate time to do the fun things you've been wanting to do, and to the activities that will move you closer to your personal and professional goals. You've earned those additional hours at considerable effort; make sure you use them well.

TIME LOG

The time log is the most valuable single tool ever devised for getting control of time. It isn't intended as part of your permanent routine, only as a diagnostic technique to be used every few months or whenever effectiveness seems to be slipping. It's easier than it looks.

Make a chart similar to the one on page 107, adapted to your own situation. Note that it is a double-entry system, with two categories: "Activity" (the things you do) and "Business Function" (the purpose for doing them). For each fifteen-minute period during the day, you put two check marks on the log, one under each category. And where needed, indicate under "Notes" exactly what you were doing.

Tape the time log to the sliding work shelf you have on your desk so it will be out of sight except when you are using it. Then, every half-hour or so (but no less often than each hour), bring it up to date. The cumulative time it will take to do this for the entire day will be perhaps three or four minutes. But the results will be astounding.

You will find that you had no idea where your time is really going. Memory is notoriously unreliable in this area because we tend to remember the highlights of the day—the moments when we were accomplishing something—and we overlook the time that was wasted or ineffectively used. The trivial items, the minor distractions, are too unimportant to be remembered. Yet these are the items we most want to identify.

After keeping a log for two or three days, you will be struck with the opportunities for improvement. For example, you probably will find you spend far more time than you realized reading trade publications, newspapers, reports, and so on, and will be motivated to find a way to cut down on this activity. You may be surprised

TIME LOG

Time	Reading	Dictation	Paperwork	Phone Calls	Consultations	Meetings	Inspections	Travel Time	Planning	Other	Sales	Purchasing	Production	Finance	Personnel	Customer Relations	Admin Routine	Other	Notes
8:00– 8:15										X								X	CHATTING
8:15– 8:30	X																X		INCOMING MAIL
8:30– 8:45		X															X		MAIL
8:45– 9:00				X														X	MISC. Phone Calls
9:00– 9:15	X																X		READING NEWSPAPER
9:15– 9:30	X																X		READING TRADE JOURNALS
9:30– 9:45										X							X		COFFEE BREAK
9:45–10:00										X							X		COFFEE BREAK
10:00–10:15			X													X			ACME – WARRANTY Problem
10:15–10:30				X												X			SAW RICHARDSON Re ACME
10:30–10:45				X												X			
10:45–11:00			X						X								X		WORK ON SALARY SCHEDULE
11:00–11:15	X								X								X		
11:15–11:30	X														X				WEEKLY REPORT
11:30–11:45			X				X												OFFICE MACHINE SALESMAN
11:45–12:00					X													X	To LUNCH WITH RICHARDSON
12:00–12:15			X											X					LUNCH " "
12:15–12:30			X											X					" " "
12:30–12:45			X											X					" " "
12:45– 1:00			X																" " "
1:00– 1:15								X										X	RETURN TO OFFICE
1:15– 1:30		X															X		RETURNED VARIOUS PHONE CALLS
1:30– 1:45		X															X		
1:45– 2:00			X														X		MET WITH BOSS
2:00– 2:15			X														X		" "
2:15– 2:30						X											X		PERSONAL ERRANDS
2:30– 2:45						X											X		" "
2:45– 3:00								X									X		TRAVEL TO SEE JOHNSON
3:00– 3:15				X									X						JOHNSON MEETING
3:15– 3:30				X									X						" "
3:30– 3:45						X											X		RETURN
3:45– 4:00						X											X		CHAT WITH ROGERS
4:00– 4:15	X																X		DICTATION ON SALARY SCHEDULE
4:15– 4:30	X																X		P.M. NEWSPAPER
4:30– 4:45			X														X		SAW MURPHY RE NEW PROCEDURES
4:45– 5:00			X														X		" " "
TOTAL	1	:30	:45	1	:4	:40	0		0	:1:30	:15	:75	:30	:30	1:52	:14			

107

at the amount of time spent traveling to appointments and will work to consolidate travel time through better scheduling or through greater use of the phone. You may find that your fifteen-minute coffee break runs more like forty minutes, counting from the time you leave your desk to go to the coffee shop until the time you get back. Maybe it's worth it, but you really can't judge until you see written evidence of exactly how much time is involved.

Most important of all, however, you will be surprised at the small percentage of your time you actually spend on what you would admit are your top-priority items, how little time you spend planning, anticipating problems, exploiting opportunities, and working toward major goals, compared to the amount of time you spend putting out fires and doing routine low-priority tasks. A time log has the same effect as a dash of cold water on your face in the morning; it's a bit unpleasant for a moment, but it wakes you up and gets you started.

It takes a bit of self-discipline to undertake the making and keeping of a time log, but I can promise you that (1) it will take far less time than you would think to keep one for a few days, and (2) it is bound to point you toward important improvements in the way you spend your time. Start one today.

A refinement of the time log idea is a device recently invented by Swedish management consultant Hans Hindersson, which is being marketed in the United States by Extensor Corporation of Minneapolis. It is a combination signal generator and recording system. At random intervals, usually about thirty times during a working day, it emits a barely audible beep and flashes a light, at which time the user punches a computer card with a stylus, responding to a number of questions with precoded answers. The questions include such things as *What are you doing now?* (The answers, tailored to the specific work of the person involved, might include such things as working on Project A, working on Project B, preparing inventory forms, handling payroll matters, reading mail, answering mail, reading the newspaper, chatting, attending a meeting, etc. There is no limit to the number of answers.) *What is the object of what you are doing?* (Sales, service, handling orders, budgeting, personnel management, relaxation, etc.) *Who initiated the action in which you are now involved?* (Self, immediate superior, subordinate, customer, visitor, etc.) *If you are communicating, what method are you using?* (Phone, writing, personal conference, meeting.) *On a scale of 1 to 5, what is your mood right now?* (This is useful for identifying activities that are troublesome and need further analysis to determine whether they should be delegated or eliminated or restructured in some way.)

After several days the technique becomes so automatic that you can punch the cards with scarcely a pause in your work. After five weeks, the cards are fed into a computer that analyzes in several different ways the patterns of time use and pinpoints various problems and opportunities for improvement.

For those who can afford it, this is the ultimate answer to the problem of finding out where time goes. For most people, however, a time log provides an adequate basis for self-analysis and pays rich rewards in improving time use.

TIME MANAGEMENT AND YOUR HEART

In their book *Type A Behavior and Your Heart*, Drs. Meyer Friedman and Ray H. Rosenman describe the kind of person they have found most likely to have coronary heart disease. They conclude that it is the kind of person who exhibits a "Type A Behavior Pattern," which they describe as "an action-emotion complex that can be observed in any person who is *aggressively* involved in a *chronic, incessant* struggle to achieve more and more in less and less time, and if required to do so, against the opposing efforts of other things or other persons."*

They go on to explain that "the fundamental sickness of the Type A subject consists of his peculiar failure to perceive, or perhaps worse, to accept the simple fact that a man's time can be exhausted by his activities. As a consequence, he never ceases trying to 'stuff' more and more events in his constantly shrinking reserves of time."

This driving sense of time urgency, according to Drs. Friedman and Rosenman, not only prevents full enjoyment of life, but also triggers physiological reactions that lead to coronary heart disease.

* Meyer Friedman and Ray H. Rosenman, *Type A Behavior and Your Heart* (New York: Alfred A. Knopf, 1974), p. 84.

If you are reading this book because you are a Type A person who wants to become more so, who wants to cram more frantic activity into every second, I hope you will realize by now that I don't think that's the way to live a fuller life. The concept of working "smarter, not harder" involves shedding such unprofitable behavior patterns as wheel-spinning, perfectionism, failure to delegate, inability to set priorities, and going through life without having established realistic goals.

Good time management will permit you to find some time each day to devote to what Drs. Friedman and Rosenman call "things worth being" rather than just "things worth having": time for reading, meditation, exercise, relaxation, solitude, and for social contacts unrelated to business. For many people this means a whole new dimension to living. For health as well as happiness it's worth a try.

TIME, SCHEDULING

Unless you are in some profession such as dentistry or psychiatry, where you can largely control your time, it doesn't make sense to make a detailed plan of how you are going to spend each minute of the day. Interruptions and unforeseen events are sure to demolish any schedule you might make up, and the result is that you get discouraged and give up planning.

Still, you do need to plan. The key to successful planning is, in the words of management consultant Peter Drucker, to schedule time "in large chunks." Allocate blocks of time to the one or two really important things you must get done during the day, and leave plenty of unscheduled time for visitors, phone calls, unforeseen emergencies, and secondary tasks.

TRANQUILLITY

The human spirit has a need for periods of quiet, solitude, and peace, when you can forget the pressures of competition and the demands of family and friends, and experience the healing power of tranquillity.

How do you find time for such moments in today's busy world? The same way you find time for anything else in life that's worthwhile: you plan for it, you set a time for it, and then you do it. Your best bet is to do it daily.

One method that has become popular in recent years is transcendental meditation (TM), which involves sitting quietly for twenty minutes twice a day, eyes closed, letting the mind wander where it will, while silently repeating a *mantra*, a Sanskrit word that sounds like a nonsense syllable. Many who practice TM report that it seems to make them more alert and less tense, and there is little question that during meditation certain physiological phenomena occur, including changes in oxygen consumption, brain waves, and blood lactate.* Whether the benefits of TM might be obtained just as well by other techniques is still an open question, but as one critic of TM has conceded, "Something that can get us to *stop* for a few minutes can't be all bad."†

But there are other ways of stopping. If you are religious, you may gain the same kind of inner peace from prayer, or from religious meditation in a church, cathedral, or synagogue, or in your own home. (One of the advantages of arising earlier than others in your household is the opportunity it provides for a few minutes each morning for solitude and reflection.) For some, sitting alone for a few minutes in a park or even a hotel lobby or a parked automobile can restore a feeling of inner calm.

Whatever method you use, try to find one or two brief periods during each day when you get away from the rat race, stand back, and get some perspective on what you are doing. It can give you the objectivity you need to sweep away some of the trivia and irrelevancies in your life when you get back to work.

* Gary E. Schwartz, "TM Relaxes Some People and Makes Them Feel Better," *Psychology Today* (April 1974), p. 40.
† Colin Campbell, "Transcendence Is as American as Ralph Waldo Emerson," *Psychology Today* (April 1974), p. 38.

UNFINISHED BUSINESS

In baseball, victory is determined not by hits but by runs. The player who gets to third base and no farther doesn't get credit for three-quarters of a run.

It's that way with a task. Getting started is fine, and carrying it forward is fine, but until the task is completed you haven't done what you set out to do. Yet many people form the habit of "working for a while" on a project, then setting it aside, kidding themselves into thinking that they have accomplished something. All they are doing is leaving men stranded on base!

This wastes time because (1) often you won't return to the task, so the time spent is lost, or (2) when you do return you have to take time to build up momentum again, retrace steps, review what was done, and get thoughts and papers in order.

Once you start something, finish it. Don't accumulate a backlog of half-finished projects.

Of course, this advice is impossible to follow when the task is too large to be completed at one time. How do you handle those situations?

Simple. You divide and conquer. Break the task down into small, manageable segments (preferably in writing), and assign yourself to complete action on one segment before stopping. Then, instead of feeling that you are leaving a lot of loose ends when you put the task aside, you will feel that you have completed one phase of the project and are ready to begin the next.

(This is essentially the "salami technique" discussed under "Procrastination.")

Suppose, for example, that you have a lengthy report to prepare. Avoid thinking in terms of "working on it for an hour or so." Instead, assign yourself the task of completing the outline or finishing the research or writing the introduction. Then, when you have done so, you will be able to put it aside with a feeling of having accomplished something specific, and with a clear idea of what the next step will be. You will avoid the mental block that comes when you have loose ends to gather up and sort out before you can start again.

By segmenting tasks you can thus develop that precious habit known as the *compulsion to closure*. It will save time for you every day.

UPWARD DELEGATION

Delegation involves giving subordinates assignments commensurate with their abilities and their duties, together with the authority to get the job done. Too often the process is reversed, and a subordinate gives the boss back a partially finished job that should have been completed at the lower level. This not only causes the boss to do things which somebody else ought to be doing, but also prevents the subordinate from growing. And the subordinate's growth is essential if the boss is to get work done and take on more responsibility.

In a *Harvard Business Review* article, William Oncken, Jr., and Donald L. Wass give a perceptive analysis of what they call "subordinate-imposed time":

> Let us imagine that a manager is walking down the hall and that he notices one of his subordinates, Mr. A, coming up the hallway. When they are abreast of one another, Mr. A greets the manager with, "Good morning. By the way, we've got a problem. You see . . ." As Mr. A continues, the manager recognizes in this problem the same two characteristics common to all the problems his subordinates gratuitously bring to his attention. Namely, the manager knows (a) enough to get involved, but (b) not enough to make the on-the-spot decision expected of him. Eventually, the manager says, "So glad you brought this up. I'm in a rush right now. Meanwhile, let me think about it and I'll let you know." Then he and Mr. A part company.
>
> Let us analyze what has just happened. Before the two of them met, on whose back was the "monkey"? The subordinate's. After they parted, on whose back was it? The manager's. Subordinate-imposed time begins the moment a monkey successfully executes a leap from the back of a subordinate to the back of his superior and does not end until the monkey is returned to its proper owner for care and feeding.*

* William Oncken, Jr., and Donald L. Wass, "Management Time: Who's got the Monkey?", *Harvard Business Review* (November–December 1974), p. 76.

The commonest form of upward delegation is the submission of partially completed work by workers who count on their superiors to make the tough decisions or put on the finishing touches or check for possible errors. When a subordinate gets away with this, it is usually because the boss believes that he or she can finish the job easier and faster. This may be true. But the job of the manager is to manage, not to do someone else's work.

The only way to end upward delegation is to toss the ball right back to your subordinates. When they habitually come to you with problems and ask you to make a decision, simply ask, "Which course do you think would be better?" Force them to make decisions (or at least firm recommendations) themselves, and unless some very serious mistake is likely, don't second-guess them.

Incidentally, if subordinates make a habit of leaving all the decisions up to you it may be because you are forcing them to do so. Ask yourself whether you are giving them the *authority* to do whatever needs to be done. If not, you can't blame them for running back to you with half-solved problems.

And remember: a good executive is someone who always has a worried look—on an assistant's face!

WASTEBASKETRY

If your office is typical, roughly three-quarters of the items to be found in your files should have been placed in your wastebasket. Insufficient use of the wastebasket leads to crowded files, a chaotic desk, an overworked file clerk, and a cluttered mind.

Be ruthless in channeling paper into the wastebasket instead of into the files. Never file memos, for example, that are routine and are on file somewhere else in the organization—such things as, for example, announcements of meetings, directives that have been superseded, press releases from other departments, house organs, and so on. File only things that you are likely to refer to again and that are not available elsewhere.

If you find that the volume of material going into your wastebasket is large, look for ways to cut off part of the stream before it reaches your desk. Perhaps your secretary can divert part of the flow directly to the wastebasket, to keep junk mail out of your "In" box.

Ask to have your name removed from mailing lists for little-read periodicals and from the routing list for office correspondence that has no value for you. Nothing is more ridiculous than to have to read a piece of paper to determine whether you ought to be reading it at all!

WEEKENDS

Protect your weekends. Don't let work spill over into weekends except in emergencies—if God needed a rest after working six days, who are you to think you can manage without a change of pace?

A weekend of exercise and relaxation, completely removed from the cares of the office or factory, can contribute to effective use of time during the week ahead. If you can occasionally schedule a long weekend, do it.

Plan your weekends, don't just take them as they come, or you will find yourself winding up a captive of the boob tube. Having specific plans for an upcoming weekend is a morale booster for the entire preceding week and provides an incentive for getting the week's work done in time so that it won't interfere with those plans.

WHEEL-SPINNING

A sure symptom of poor time use is the mad scramble of activity that results from a poor job of goal-setting, planning, and delegating.

Working frantically in a crisis atmosphere seldom produces satisfactory results. The old maxim of the Pennsylvania Dutch, "The hurrieder I go, the behinder I get," pretty well sums up the situation.

Instead of spinning your wheels when you are faced with a crisis, take the actions that you should have taken to prevent yourself from getting there in the first place: stop and clarify your objective, take stock of your resources, delegate whatever can be delegated, set a firm list of priorities and stick to them, try to forestall interruptions, and then start working on the item that is number one on your priority list.

After you have worked your way out of the crisis, sit down and ask yourself why it happened and what you can do to prevent its recurrence in the future.

WORDS TO WORK BY

Perhaps the most valuable result of all education is the ability to make yourself do the thing you have to do when it ought to be done, whether you like it or not; it is the first lesson that ought to learned; and however early a man's training begins, it is probably the last lesson that he learns thoroughly.

—Thomas Huxley

The world is cluttered up with unfinished business in the form of projects that might have been successful, if only at the tide point someone's patience had turned to active impatience.

—Robert Updegraff

Many of us spend half our time wishing for things we could have if we didn't spend half our time wishing.

—Alexander Woollcott

Whenever you can save some of your time by offering money in its place, do so. Strangely, from their earliest beginnings men have always seemed quite happy to trade the very limited days of their lives for disks of copper, bronze, silver, and gold.

—Meyer Friedman, M.D., and
Ray H. Rosenman, M.D.

It is more important to do the right thing than to do things right.

—Peter Drucker

WORKAHOLIC

People can become addicted to work just as they can become addicted to alcohol. Symptoms of this addiction include refusal to take a vacation, inability to put the office out of your mind on weekends, a bulging briefcase full of work, and a son or a daughter whose face is familiar, but you can't recall the name.*

This syndrome can result from either of two things. The first is simply an inability to get on top of the job because of ineffective use of time (failure to establish priorities, wheel-spinning, inefficient delegation, procrastination, etc.). In this case, the techniques discussed in this book can solve the problem. The second is a subconscious *desire* to be snowed under by work and to stay that way. This may be the result of a wish to escape from an unpleasant home life, of a martyr complex, of a desire to appear indispensable, of a realization that you don't have a repertoire of leisure activities that provide satisfaction and enjoyment.

Whatever the reason, a person in this situation

---

* It should be noted that working long hours does not necessarily mean you are a work addict. As a matter of fact, although a few executives work forty hours or less per week, most of the successful ones I know average considerably more than that. What differentiates them from the "workaholic" is that (1) they use their time well in achieving objectives, instead of getting their kicks from the activity itself; and (2) they don't let work interfere with the really important things in life, such as friends, family, and fly fishing.

clearly is concerned with *activities* (staying busy) rather than *achievements* (getting things done). Counseling can help such people cope with their problems, and it is unfortunate that so many fail to consult a psychologist or psychiatrist or psychotherapist until things reach a crisis point.

But for starters, do a bit of self-counseling. Read the section on goals, and ask yourself honestly what your lifetime goals are and whether the things you are now doing are really moving you toward them. Ask yourself honestly where health stands in your list of priorities, whether the midnight oil you are burning is adversely affecting it, and whether that is an acceptable price. Ask where your family comes in your list of priorities, whether you are giving enough of yourself to your children and your spouse, and whether you are deceiving yourself by pretending that the sacrifices you are making are really for them.

Then plan to meet your wife or your husband for lunch next Tuesday, and to take your children to the zoo next Thursday afternoon. You owe it to them, and to yourself.

A FINAL WORD

Above all else, good time management involves an awareness that today is all we ever have to work with. The past is irretrievably gone, the future is only a concept. Everything that is accomplished in the world is the result of someone's realization that today is the only time to act.

If that seems rather elementary to you, be assured that the vast majority of your fellow human beings seldom fully grasp that self-evident truth.

Thomas Carlyle put it this way: "Our main task is not to see what lies dimly perceived in the future, but to do the thing which lies immediately at hand." John Ruskin had the word "TODAY" carved into a small marble block that he kept on his desk as a constant reminder to "Do It Now."

But my favorite quotation is this one by an anonymous philosopher:

> YESTERDAY is a cancelled check.
> TOMORROW is a promissory note.
> TODAY is ready cash. Use it!

DOING IT NOW

Edwin C Bliss

Do you always put off that difficult decision? Postpone cleaning out your cupboards? Forget to buy the paint the bedroom's crying out for? Think about all the things you're putting off at home, at work, in your personal relationships – and then look around you. You'll see that *successful* people *never* procrastinate: they always do things *now*.

DO IT NOW!

Edwin Bliss's realistic approach to the problem shows you how to succeed in whatever goals you set up for yourself. Once you've overcome whatever is holding you back – whether it's shyness, fear of success, depression, indecision, clutter, fatigue or stress – you'll find your life is fuller, more satisfying – and much more enjoyable.

DOING IT NOW – a book that will change your life.

Futura Publications
Non-Fiction
0 7088 2600 8

MEGATRENDS
Ten new directions transforming our lives

John Naisbitt

Using techniques of newspaper analysis first devised in World War II, John Naisbitt looks at ten observable trends observable in today's world and predicts the developments of the future. A primer for the eighties that shows just where our sophisticated technology is taking us, he points to the shifts from industrial society to information society, from centralization to decentralization, from institutional help to self-help and advises us how we can adapt to and capitalise on them.

'John Naisbitt is one of the shrewdest observers of the changes sweeping America today'
Alvin Toffler, author of FUTURE SHOCK.

'A thoughtful work which makes a plea for technology on a human scale'
The Guardian

Futura Publications
Non-Fiction
0 7088 2508 7

**THE SUPERWOMAN TRAP –
and HOW TO ESCAPE IT**

Cathy Douglas

She's smart, she's successful and she can turn a hand
to anything from haute couture and haute cuisine to
changing a spark plug or redesigning the house. In
between running a busy office and producing home-
made tomato chutney, she has multiple orgasms and
reads all the right books . . .

She's Superwoman. And she doesn't exist, except in
the pages of glossy magazines – and in the frustrated
ambitions of millions of modern women. THE
SUPERWOMAN TRAP is a new form of oppression,
setting an unattainable goal and producing guilt and
misery in those who strive for it.

In this timely, wise and witty book Cathy Douglas takes
a sardonic look at the myth and the reality of
Superwoman – and shows you how to cock a snook
at the tyranny of perfection and live the life *you* want
to.

Futura Publications
Non-Fiction
0 7088 2647 4

U & NON-U REVISITED

Edited by Richard Buckle

A Classic Compendium for all those who wish to be in the U-know!

A generation after Nancy Mitford first stirred the drawing rooms of Great Britain into social debate with her demarcation lines of U and Non-U, the new standard was announced by Professor Alan Ross and his team of social luminaries.

Bringing a touch of fresh courage to all those who agonised over what they could say and when, and whether they could ever be 'pleased to meet you', and introducing the DOUBLE U!

The book no self-respecting socialite should be without!

'Fascinating reading'
Evening News

Futura Publications
Non-Fiction/Humour
0 7088 1766 1

DANGER! MEN AT WORK

Rosalind Miles

HOW TO MAKE IT IN A MAN'S WORLD

So you think the battle for sexual equality is over and won? That new laws have made the workplace a paradise of female opportunity? Think again!

It's more like a jungle where you're in constant danger from hostile natives, and likely to experience

★ SEXUAL HARASSMENT
★ DELIBERATE DISCRIMINATION
★ LACK OF TRAINING
★ BARRIERS TO PROMOTION

But don't despair! The wind of change is blowing up the trouserlegs of the male powerholders. Women everywhere are taking a long cool look at their situation and refusing to accept the status quo. And here is a vital handbook to help you on the way.

Wise, witty, well-informed, often irreverent, always positive — this is the indispensable guide through the minefield of the workplace.

So get out there and at 'em — you've nothing to lose but your chains.

Futura Publications
Non-Fiction/General
0 7088 2371 8

BIO-RHYTHM 1983-84-85
A Personal Science

Bernard Gittelson

Learn how to chart your natural body cycles so you can plan your life with confidence, maximise the best and minimise the worst of the ups and downs of life.

Using our newest scientific discipline, the computerized study of biological clocks — built-in natural cycles that powerfully influence our behaviour, you can accurately forecast what life has in store for you.

Construct your own biorhythm chart from the simple and easy-to-use tables in the book and begin to benefit from your BIORHYTHM!

Futura Publications
Non-Fiction
0 7088 2290 8

NOBLESSE OBLIGE

Edited by Nancy Mitford

With illustrations by Osbert Lancaster

The ORIGINAL book of U and Non-U that first ignited the fires of the Great Debate – that had society ladies shaking over their sherry glasses, found the stolid gentlemen of the Clubs choking over their cigars, caused certain unpleasant incidents in the Guards and promoted acrimonious correspondence in *The Times*.

Edited by the inimitable Nancy Mitford and with her own firebrand essay on the lethal; implications of Usage – sweet or pudding? – and including the unique and various talents of:

★ Professor Alan Ross with his famous (or infamous) essay on U and Non-U language and class

★ Evelyn Waugh on the Great U Debate

★ John Betjeman on 'How to Get on in Society'

Futura Publications
Non-Fiction/Humour
0 7088 2768 8

All Futura Books are available at your bookshop or newsagent, or can be ordered from the following address:
Futura Books, Cash Sales Department,
P.O. Box 11, Falmouth, Cornwall TR10 9EN.

Please send cheque or postal order (no currency), and allow 60p for postage and packing for the first book plus 25p for the second book and 15p for each additional book ordered up to a maximum charge of £1.90 in U.K.

B.F.P.O. customers please allow 60p for the first book, 25p for the second book plus 15p per copy for the next 7 books, thereafter 9p per book.

Overseas customers including Eire please allow £1.25 for postage and packing for the first book, 75p for the second book and 28p for each subsequent title ordered.